# About th

The author grew up in a mixed religious community in Derry during the Troubles. He often questioned the British Protestant ideology and culture that he was indoctrinated into and in his teens began to explore the sense of Irish culture and history available to him, through its music and stories. To escape the Troubles, he left for mainland Britain in 1981 aged nineteen. He studied as a mature student in southern England and eventually moved to Cardiff in South Wales. His careers as a college lecturer in English, a therapist (still is) and a manager of a university wellbeing service gave him an insight to human behaviour, the human psyche and the complexity of family relationships. It also encouraged him to spend much time in self-reflection — which became the drive to writing the memoirs of his childhood years.

# OVER THE TINS

# Sid Kennedy

OVER THE TINS

Vanguard Press

VANGUARD PAPERBACK

A CIP catalogue record for this title is
available from the British Library.

ISBN 978-1-80016-035-4

*Vanguard Press is an imprint of
Pegasus Elliot MacKenzie Publishers Ltd.*
www.pegasuspublishers.com

First Published in 2021

**Vanguard Press
Sheraton House Castle Park
Cambridge England**

Printed & Bound in Great Britain

# Dedication

To Ma, the greatest of storytellers.

# Acknowledgements

I would like to thank a number of people who have made this book possible.

My mother, for keeping the past alive with her continual telling of stories of family life and who, unknowingly, passed on her gift to me.

My wife Julie, whose constancy and encouragement gave me the confidence and courage to write the first and last words of this book.

My son, Piers, and daughter, Lara, whose sensitive and constructive feedback on my drafts, allowed me to really 'see' what I had written.

My publisher, who had enough faith in my first attempt at writing, to print it.

My siblings, Mina, Irene, Robin, Hazel, Val, Paul and Issi, who helped to sculpture the person I am.

My father, who worked tirelessly to ensure the Kennedy family had a home, were always clothed and never went hungry.

# Chapter One
## The Beginning of it all

'Twins. It's twins. Twin boys.'

    'Oh me God!'

    'Jesus!'

    'Aw, bless.'

A wave of wonder and disbelief spread over the Four Streets of three-bedroomed terraced houses, as news of our birth was first brought from the hospital by our da. No one knew, not even me ma, that twins were due, hence the exclusive qualities of our beginning. To those of the Four Streets, worldly news was much less important than a good old gossipy topic such as this. Chinese whisperers could do a grand job on the first twins born in the neighbourhood, let alone the fact that Minnie and Bertie already had five mouths to cater for. The previous five were 'home births', therefore their news was on the doorstep and hot off the press to everyone's lips. Having to wait for news of us being born at the hospital meant that there were many-a-folded-arm on many-a-polished-doorstep, tense with anticipation of Da's grey and white Morris Oxford easing down the steep hill of Alfred Street. Living at the bottom house only heightened the drama. As Da always loved playing the role of the oracle and focus of attention, the car never moved out of second gear — the speed was more fitting for a funeral procession than that of the triumphant revelation he was about to share.

This near-celeb status certainly had its pros and cons — though cons would win the duel. The first con was the fact that Paul had all the cooing and purring from family, friends, foes and hangers-on as he arrived home a couple of days before I did. A bruised shoulder inflicted in the womb (no guesses who did the inflicting) kept me under the 'play-safe' hospital doctor's eye. The first pro was having oodles of sympathy and cwtching (Welsh for cuddles I've since learned) fit for a victim of bullying. Rife rivalry between us had only just begun — I blame Kennedy genetics, as competition was the one trait that all eight of us siblings fiercely displayed, and still do.

Up till I had mastered a nifty sense of mobility I clearly played second fiddle on the competition front with me twin. Whether it be drinking milk from the bottle, sucking the crust of an unsliced white loaf, gulping spoonful's of colcannon, sleeping soundly throughout the day or night (probably a reflection of a well-fed tummy) or dominating space in the pram and cot, the *other twin* won hands down. In fact, I also lost out on the bonny baby beauty contest as fat babies were seen as the healthier, and indeed, in strangely 'Christian' terms, more heavenly. I think the healthier criterion is the one that still irks. Cruelly ironic is the fact that I was to become the podgier one forty years later and labelled the less healthy one — where's the justice in that?

So it was well overdue when I fired the arrow of payback — it was really more like hundreds of arrows reminiscent of Robin Hood's ever-abundant supply. Only me deeds were not of so morally high a ground as Robin's, but more of the Dick Dastardly variety where to win at any cost to the recipient was paramount. A frequently told story (one me ma enjoyed reciting to all and sundry for years) of one of me early deeds involved the playpen. In fact, this one event epitomised many others, as it had its roots in the contrast in physique between me and Paul (that's the other half). In plain terms it represented the rascality of me nimble, quick-footed and energetic skinny frame and the innocence of Paul's static, ponderous and well-rounded one.

I was able to hold on to the faded blue, wooden-framed playpen and bounce up and down at a velocity well beyond that fit for one of twenty months. I'm sure only Donegal boxing maestro Barry McGuigan in his heyday matched such a skinny frame with similar force. Knowing now that the toddler cage had previously penned in me much older brother and four older sisters in the years before us, it was a miracle that the poor old thing didn't throw in the towel and collapse in a heap of well-beaten rods. Such sturdiness deserves the clichéd cries of 'things were made to last in those days' — I'm not going to be drawn into that time-worn discussion

13

just yet. Having vibrated the thing across the linoleum kitchen (the main room) flooring about three feet until it bumped up against the shiny red sofa, I was then able to use the low seating of this to clamber out to Braveheartesque 'freeeeeeeedom'. Not so for the still-captive Paul. As he feebly attempted to follow suit I devilishly and silently pulled his ears in total ignorance of the pain it bore on his rounded head. There's something ruthlessly primitive about inflicting anguish on the vulnerable and taking satisfaction in the process until we grow out of it or a sense of reasoning overpowers it. Being a mere toddler meant there was no hope for Paul — the more he wailed the more I rejoiced and therefore the more ear-pulling was dished out.

An adult to observe such animalistic behaviour usually sends them into a rage that is, too reminiscent of our Stone Age ancestors, and a disgust that reflects how civilised we have now become. Both emotions probably feed each other. The adult in today's non-smacking society is left with suppressing such strong inner turmoil and to displace this later in the day over something remotely trivial. However, the adult in sixties Derry had no hesitation of unleashing that fury-filled feeling on the wrongdoer and to give them their just desserts — a whacking. Its sole intention would be to simply teach them right from wrong and to hopefully ensure that such behaviour would not be repeated.

Enter into the ring, Ma — though Da could just as ably be the educator with his own brand of teaching

14

methodology. Rawhide bare hands with a velocity that made me earlier force minuscule in comparison, landing on me unsunned, soft and skinny legs, clearly left their mark. It's uncanny that the punishment bit is usually edited out of glorified storytelling; the finger of innate parental guilt seems to timely press the edit button when the nostalgic stories are being replayed. I suppose that allows for focus on the guilty party being the initial 'sinner'. I still get stick for me crime forty years on, so me penitence lives on. There's a fuller version of this later in the book, so this is just to whet your appetite!

Ma and Da's teaching of morality was without question, typical of our locale. To hear a child's screams and wails behind a heavy wooden front door meant one of two things — either an older sibling had tapped into their primitive psyche and be bullying a younger sibling, or a parent was carrying out their rightful duty to educate the values and norms that Derry folk agreed upon. I say Derry folk, yet ironically, neither of me parents came from Derry; the cultural curriculum was obviously the same in Derry as in other parts of Ireland too.

Ma originated from Northern Ireland — the bit of luscious agricultural land that somehow tags itself on to the realms of the United Kingdom; the bit that means that you are British yet not part of Great Britain; the bit that means you are Irish yet part of the British Isles. Identity crises seem part and parcel of this part of the world — it gets worse when you move across the Irish

Sea as I experienced many years later. Da came from the Republic of Ireland — or as those dedicated to Irish Nationalism like to refer to it, Eire. On the other hand, we children from the North were taught to call it the Free State. The word Free had its obvious connotations to us innocent kids, yet its political reference was neither taught nor explained — even if it had it would have been lost on us anyway. Politics was going to be left for us to find out about ourselves — what a journey that turned out to be. Looking back now I think I prefer the childish innocence or mass oblivion of it all — there were certainly no answers to be had from no questions.

# Chapter Two
# Ma

Ma entered the world and grew up in a little country location called Drumalief in County Derry; the nearest small settlement was Limavady, about sixteen miles north of Derry. Drumalief was one of those places that really baffled me in terms of its geographical location — when do you know that you are in it or when you are out of it? It was just as well I wasn't doing demographic research of the area during one of me frequent visits there as a child to visit me granny, me Uncle Billy and Aunt Jean — me methodology would have been quite unique though. For years there was no road sign indicating that 'this' was Drumalief. In fact, I thought for years that Granny's actual dirty red brick house was *it*, but this idea was also confusing because the house was adjoined at the hip, chest and head to another one. They both couldn't have the same name could they? What was the other called? Years later I wondered why the hell in the middle of nowhere were there two houses built together in the first place; no other dwelling in twenty miles was like it. Ma and Da never had the answers to intriguing questions so I gave up asking them. They never gave the answers to any questions —

Truth.

Over the years as the number of vehicles increased, as more remote places became less obscure and insular, and as the tourist industry spread its all-encompassing wings of change, road signs were installed at either end of the road on which stood the red house. This gave some idea of location but one straightish line on a map didn't create a boundary; where were all the other boundaries? Did specific hedgerows known only by locals represent territory demarcation? Of course, this fixation of mine led to similar ones as Ireland was predominantly fields, hills and mountains with the odd village, town or big town (Derry and Belfast were merely big towns to me) dotted in amongst this vast expanse of sloping shades of green fabric. Everywhere I went beyond the boundaries of Derry in the car, led to the obsession of locating where one area ended and another began. I even imagined that *this* place started along *this* line of trees and ended along *that* line of brambly mass. I'm not surprised I dropped geography in form three at secondary school. Me reason at the time was "I just don't like it", but it was obviously me subconscious security network stepping in to avoid obsessive compulsive disorder later in life — at least on this front anyway. On an ironically positive note, place-name questions when playing Trivial Pursuit in the years to come often resulted in me being awarded with a triangular piece of yellow plastic — all that self-educating obviously paid off.

Ma was undoubtedly a country girl whose experience of life beyond Limavady to the south and Coleraine to the north was limited. Being one of seven children meant that she was able to rely on her three brothers and three sisters for fun, fights, friendship and foes. Her school friendships were more or less confined to the tiny eighteenth-century playground in Limavady, although there was some craic to be had on the three-mile walk to get there and back. Ma loved to boast about this walking feat in all weathers — it was like an indirect criticism of how the next generation and its cultural pathways were of lesser value to her own (is this superior way of thinking how we all turn out eventually?) Her lack of directness always meant that we all had to gauge the inference; though that certainly changed as she reached the latter years of her life! Ma would doubt our interpretation of what she inferred and then the bubble of suppressing her opinions (in general) would finally burst, and she would metaphorically hit you directly in the middle of your forehead. Once the bubble of restraint burst, she'd lose all compassion regarding its outcome — more often than not, humiliating or embarrassing the recipient! It was safer to follow such situations with a degree of silence, without comeback of a supposed interpretation.

There was no need for the Green Cross Code man on her school route as traffic of any note or speeding beyond tractors hadn't been conceived in that remote part of the world. Ten-mile charity walks would have been a mere doddle, while forty-mile ones would have been a half decent challenge. I'm not surprised then that there was no such thing as charity fundraising in those days as nobody would have wanted to sponsor you for a five-kilometre walk! With this amount of trekking it was just as well that the likes of me granda, and men of his time and place, were 'jacks of all trades' and able to mend the soles of their family's shoes. It was not surprising then that keeping the toes of a shoe from the curse of a hole was paramount to the mortality of the shoe itself. The uppers were not as easy to mend as the soles, so any child scuffing at stones or the ground would bring upon themselves a severe reprimand from an adult, regardless if they were related to you or not. If Ma did something that her own ma and da disapproved of then any other adult reinforcing *their* 'rules' were well within their remit to do so.

Apart from siblings, Ma had a few farm animals to keep her company. Her da had created a smallholding that was typical of the area — one cow, a dozen chickens and a couple of pigs. I know, though, that despite being a country lass, Ma had little or nothing to do with them. Throughout her life animals were certainly not her thing, which is probably why she would chase cats away from our concrete backyard in Alfred Street armed with a sweeping brush with an animosity and venom fit for Joan of Arc's elimination of her adversaries. It would also explain why we never had a pet of any description despite constant requests from us wee ones. Even newts that me and Paul cleverly captured and imprisoned in jam jars were dealt the fatal verbal blow of banishment after a paltry twenty-four hours. She saw all animals as dirty, smelly and anti-hygienic — Ma was certainly not the stereotypical country girl who welcomed all things rural.

It was obvious until I was well into me teens that Ma spent more time working indoors than outdoors at Drumalief. Durkheim's division of labour was clearly visible in this rural setting (and later in the setting of Derry till the Troubles emerged) as the females did the cleaning, washing, ironing, cooking and baking, whilst the males did the mending, building, farming and the paid work. This now 'outdated' sense of family organisation seemed to work for Ma's folks' family and later for her own. It wasn't until after me da had passed away in the late eighties that Ma directly stated (told you she changed!) that she'd go out to work if she had her time on this earth over again. This confession of sacrifice and altruism clearly shook me as I had always seen Ma as extremely hardworking and tired but also *content*. To have this image of a parent firmly implanted in your psyche and then have it distorted leaves a crack of confusion and a gully of guilt in your head — as if we offspring were somehow responsible for her 'missing out' on life. Ma sure knew how to twist the knife of guilt in if she wanted to make you feel bad about yourself.

The traditional gender roles seemed fine with me

anyway. The selfish part of me was only concerned with the gorgeous baking that Ma, me aunties and me granny did on a regular basis. Drumalief tea on our Sunday visits usually consisted of salad stuff (well, by salad I mean tasteless lettuce, sliced tomato, sliced boiled egg, slices of ham, luncheon meat and corned beef) and a mouth-watering mixture of breads — wheaten, fruit, treacle and plain. They had all been freshly baked the day before by me granny and me aunt Jean in preparation for the expected extended family Sunday gathering (about twelve adults and sixteen kids), so there were never any stale bits to test the strength of your jawbone on. By the time I'd had at least one slice of each loaf followed by a couple of doorstep slices of home-baked fruit cake, and all washed down with gallons of tea (made with tea leaves and brewed on a gas ring to the colour of tar, of course), I was well and truly stuffed to the hilt. The bread was made even the tastier by the home-made jams — rhubarb, blueberry, blackberry and raspberry. These ingredients were wildly grown local produce picked by family members at different times of the year and quickly preserved in jars ready for mass consumption at any time of the year. Of course, Ma had practised the art of baking and fruit-preserving to an advanced level by the time she left Drumalief in her early twenties and was therefore able to carry on this ancestral Sherrard (maiden name) tradition with us in Derry. In fact, the good knock-on effect of visiting Drumalief was that Ma would have pangs for her roots and invariably do her own baking the following week — who needed to want for anything when they had this scrumptious bread?

Unfortunately, me own apprenticeship in baking did not go full term — mixing ingredients in a ceramic bowl with a spoon followed by a messy session of licking it out after the main contents were removed by Ma was as far as I got. Years later I eventually got Ma to perform the daunting task of writing down the ingredients for wheaten and treacle bread. The measurements were purely ad hoc as she had never used any form of measuring or weighing — the touch of a true expert. Regrettably, I misplaced this historical document, and as I couldn't face putting Ma through the turmoil of writing again, the family bread tradition as I once knew it has disappeared. I've tried the local supermarket stuff as it seems trendy for supermarkets to stock any produce with 'Irish' on the label, but although it's edible, it neither stimulates me taste buds nor me adrenalin. The same goes for Guinness out of Ireland. Guinness drinkers like me express a similar sentiment about the toned-down black stuff that's mass-produced in the breweries of mainland Britain. Its watered-down version is smoother on the palate, but is undoubtedly not the same as the real thick creamy original stuff. However, when there's no choice, then beggars can't be choosers!

So Ma's gender-role indoctrination clearly moulded her into the highly organised, practical, housekeeping Ma that I recall as a child — especially during me eleven years in Alfred Street and the Four Streets. As Da would be out of the house for nine hours a day while at work, Ma would see to us eight kids in terms of sorting breakfast, clothes, pack lunches when at school, cleaning the house, doing the washing (the twin tub washing machine couldn't have arrived quick enough when I was about eight), doing the daily shop at the local stores for tea in the evening, managing the food budget and ironing everything down to socks and underwear. The list could easily be expanded, but the Wonder Woman image is probably apparent by now. I can only guess that she learned many of her skills from her own ma.

Disciplining was not quite her forte but when called upon she could handle us kids when pushed, without the aid of Da or the threat of him. I can still hear her now saying,

"Well, I just had to discipline yees; I couldn't rely on yer da being here all the time, so I just had to do it. Sure, I couldn't have coped otherwise."

Smacks were definitely ten times worse when wearing shorts! Having to wear these till I was practically in double figures age-wise meant that me skinny legs were clearly and highly vulnerable to smacks, or a good hiding. Though Ma was perhaps not quite in the same league as Da there was still enough pain around to avoid repeating the crime that I was being punished for. The additional knowledge that it was highly probable that a second helping from Da would be dished out when he returned home from work, reinforced the learning experience intended by Ma in the first place. I'm not sure if Ma learned her disciplining skills from her own ma but I do know that I never gave me granny any grief. Granny's sudden, yet brief, change in facial expression from soft and loving to coarse and threatening was always enough to warrant conformity from all of us grandchildren. Fear has a lot to answer for. But then again, we usually treat our grandparents differently to our parents, and vice versa.

# Chapter Three
# Da

The maternal figures in me own world might have instilled fear in me but it was the paternal figures who were ultimately the kings of fear. In contrast to Ma's double-sided nature Da was singularly primitive for the majority of time. His harsh, pointed facial features, bear-like angry brow and intimidating bald head was enough to frighten the Roman-conquering Germanic Celts let alone me and Paul. I mention only the two of us as it was obvious that his patience (what little there might have been in the first place) had run dry after fathering one son and four daughters prior to us landing on his lap. His impatience was probably exacerbated by our own particular forms of devilment, adventure and energetic play. We therefore became the focus of his frustration and smouldering anger.

Although Da lived in Derry from the early stages of Hitler's onslaught on France and then died there in the year of tragic, yet less emphatic disasters, Zeebrugge and Hillsborough, he actually heralded from the small Donegal town of Letterkenny in the Free State. Unlike Drumalief, Letterkenny's boundaries were more clearly marked out on local maps of the area. However, his identity was in some ways just as blurred as those of us born in the 'British' north. Was he Irish? British? Letterkenny man? Derryman? Politics of any particular persuasion never entered his head, even during the twenty years of the Troubles he lived through, so he was happy being the Derryman when with Ma's Loyalist relatives from the north and the Donegal man when in Derry or in the Free State.

His family home in Letterkenny was a tiny, thatched-roof cottage built on a slope on the town's main street. We would pass it on family trips to the natural expansive beaches and mountainous landscape on the western side of Lough Swilly. Da would take enormous pride in always pointing it out, yet rarely talked about family life; his ma and da only got a passive mention on a rare occasion. His brief stories of long walks, very long cycle rides, apple-picking, hay-making or purdie-picking would always grab the attention. I would conjure romantic images of a world only seen in old sepia-filled photograph albums or hanging from whitewashed walls in folk museums; it all seemed so peaceful, easy and slow and I longed to experience such culture. Ironically, when leaving Ireland meself in the early eighties for the multi-cog-driven culture of mainland Britain I realised that in leaving Derry, I had left such a world in comparative terms. The contrast today of the stress-filled driver on the wide yet vehicle-packed M25 and who longs to move faster, to the ultra-chilled driver on the seemingly car-less narrow roads of the Inishowen tourist route in Donegal, and who embraces the Sunday afternoon drive mentality, is just vast. It's often not the Irish who boast of the glorious slow and calming pace of life throughout the green isle but those who have sampled a slice of its cake. I still have to diplomatically chuckle when someone meets me and tells me this as if I'd never been there. I choose not to burst their 'bubble', and instead, just quietly tell meself that I'm a crumb of that cake.

As I said, Da didn't talk about his family life to any great degree, and the fact that I never knew either of his parents as they'd died before I was born, left a strong sense of mystery and the unknown about them. The fragments of detail that I managed to hear produced the basic picture that his own da was lurch-like tall, conservative in all things, a gentleman in the eyes of others and a man who embodied a puritanical strictness. Constantly wearing a black suit with a white shirt and braces meant that he fitted in with the norm, as all men from his era and location wore the same uniform. This bleak image would fill me subconscious and embed itself in me dreams. I was a fanatical sleepwalker and prone to nightmares, at least till I left Alfred Street. I think the dark and dingy bedroom I shared with Paul, me younger sister Isobel and me parents, lit by a depressing twenty-five-watt bulb, and the fact that I slept in the lower depths of the bunk bed hemmed in by a huge oak wardrobe, accelerated me imagination to scary heights.

I would frequently 'wake up' to this dark and mysterious figure standing at the side of me bed with his face virtually hidden by a black wide-brimmed hat, but a bloodless skin could just about be made out. He wore a black three-piece suit, white shirt and black tie and stood tall and still. I would freeze, unsure if I was still breathing or not, unable to make a sound for anyone to hear. Once he left, I'd try to spring me terrified frame from the suffocating tight bedclothes of sheets and blankets, but this was a fight in itself. When I'd freed meself from the shackles of linen and wool I'd run down the stairs to find older sisters and Ma and Da watching the black and white telly as if nothing had happened. Some laughter would break from the mouths of me sisters and I felt in another world to theirs; I also felt embarrassed and humiliated. Me own mouth struggled to burble something about the great figure upstairs who had visited me for the umpteenth time. No one was really interested or concerned, but I never knew why — he was real to me; why didn't anyone believe me? Me confused head and quaking bones were given the standard half glass of milk and a rich tea biscuit to remedy their malfunctioning — they worked! I guess if I had been really clever, I could have used the 'scary man' escapades as a source of conning me way to milk and a biscuit on a more regular basis. Saying that, I couldn't have faced anything that was a stark reminder of *that* man, never mind the feelings of entrapment, asphyxiation and embarrassment.

After the commotion had finally waned, Da would take me back to bed, leave me there and I'd fall asleep after turning to face the wall, so that I wouldn't be able to see *him* if he returned. It was just as well I never got to know him in 'real' life.

Thankfully, me da's ma was a completely different person. She, I learned, was a tiny woman, warm and caring but physically weak. Her one negative trait, though, was how over-protecting she was of Da — which would at times overspill into obsessive controlling behaviour. She never appeared in any form by the side of me bed but I often wondered if she too had been scared of me da's da, but I suppose she knew parts of him he never showed me. Unfortunately, her feeble body resulted in her becoming ill at a premature age — in fact, Ma went to live with her in-laws once she married Da, in order to look after her during the last eight months in this world.

To marry a man after six months of 'courtship', to move away from everything and everyone she knew and to then look after her husband's parents after having met them only once before was a real challenge for a young woman of twenty-three to be faced with. Her words, "Well, I just got on with it" echoed her stoical attitude to life — which leaves me conscious of at least one distinct commonality that helped unite her and Da.

It was not until I was twenty and making one of me frequent visits back to Derry that Ma inadvertently and nervously told me about her mother-in-law and more about the family Da was part of. Da was out getting messages so she felt free enough to share some detail.

Da was born the youngest of eight children and was the only boy. I've seen many families where the only male child is pampered and fussed over by his sisters of often three or more. There would also be a sense of admiration and idolisation on behalf of the sisters too as the only brother became the only second 'hunter' and 'protector' in the family after their da. If the only male was also the youngest then these attitudinal qualities would be heightened. Unfortunately, in the case of Da, these relationships did not get the chance to become fully realised. The primitive health care at the time and the poverty-stricken environment that Da was born into meant that the great evils of tuberculosis, typhoid and lesser evils of mumps, measles and chickenpox swept all before them. They cruelly robbed him of all seven sisters at various stages of their short lives — some at birth, some in their early years and some in their teens. Such close proximity to death would be enough to desensitise the most emotional of characters, so it wasn't surprising that Da had a coldness that never allowed him to really emotionally attach himself to his offspring; or anyone other than Ma for that matter. He had a sense of humour that generally emerged when in adult company and he had a strong and close relationship with Ma. Although he did have fun with his children when playing board games, cards and more significantly when playing football with me and Paul, he remained to us as a figure of stone-like qualities — stubborn, strong, cold and detached. In fact, it wasn't just the loss of sisters that impacted on him, but the whole culture of premature death that surrounded his early years in remote Donegal. I guess it was a symbol of strength that he and others like him were able to live with death in the way they did and to move on and exist in the present with perhaps only a picture of the *near* future in mind.

I'm all too well aware that the fragility of mortality that Da faced had been faced by many communities, tribes and peoples across the globe and across the centuries. Reading Irish and Scottish folk stories and experiencing many literary works by the likes of Shakespeare, Tolstoy, Synge, Solzhenitsyn and Levi gave a humbling sense of how Death was a perennial and universal daily presence in others' lives. I had different fears to be concerned with when growing up but none were as lethal or as quick to impact as Lucifer and his band of renegades.

It was weird then to venture into Donegal to visit Da's relatives and only see old people. In fact, they seemed to not only still live in an era that existed decades before I vacated the womb, but also looked like wax relics in a folk museum, spoke in a rural dialect that suggested a marring and a marrying of the English and Irish languages. The atmosphere in their homes was not so much a deathly one, but one that exuded staleness, melancholy and dullness. I guess these are often facets of a deathly atmosphere too, but in these occasions a corpse was not present (well, except for one).

What an antithesis to Da's family was Ma's! She had loads of alive and kicking sisters and brothers and aunts and uncles (although I rarely set eyes on any aunts and uncles), and when the hordes got together at HQ Drumalief I'd be witness to stories of their lives and past and present. Even though adult chatter was tedious, boring and alien to me I could still hear familiar and unfamiliar names mentioned in anecdote after anecdote by the constant overlapping splashes of voices — followed by gushing waves of laughter. The sadder accounts were easily detectable by the soft murmuring voice of an individual followed by the silence of shaking heads — and then concluded by a positive tag-on such as "aye, a good man". It was easy to draw a picture of Ma's family: Granny with her pinny worn from morn till night and with her arms elbow-deep in some form of cleaning water or food ingredients, hence the massive Popeye-like forearms (who needed the shiny, chrome apparatus of today's fancy fitness gym suites to build muscles of rock in those days?); Aunt Jean with her bright humour and flirtation who was sought after by many a young farming man, yet never married any of them. Her no-holds-barred opinions were a delight amongst the conservative, taboo-ridden culture she was part of, whilst her forte to sneak up behind you to launch a womanly crunching cuddle caused a mixed dose of red-faced embarrassment and an inner warmth to stir the cockles of your soul; Uncle Billy with his constant twitching of every facial muscle that plagued him all his life and that brought ridicule from boys and rejection from girls (he, like Jean, never *did* marry, and lived together at Drumalief for donkey's years) — he did find solace in kicking a battered leather football about and collecting memorabilia about his beloved Glasgow Rangers; Uncle Aubrey, the pioneer, who was, like his da, to sample life outside of County Derry by joining the army, and who never quite connected to the others in the same way he did before he left. His less insular and philosophical outlook was not founded on any nurturing and remains one of psychology's and biology's mysteries. How can one child of seven children of the same parents and brought up with the same values, norms and outlook on life be so different? Such quandaries often lead to the good old-fashioned spinning of myths in an attempt to grasp some meaning and reasoning — usually to the detriment of the individual concerned. (The same was to occur in Ma's own family but more on that later). In Ireland such myths lacked imagination and instead were based on realism — "he was dropped on his head when just a wee baby", or "she had a fit when asleep one night when five years old and was never the same", or "he choked and choked on an apple peel till his face was purple and then he was sick — he changed from that moment on". Not surprisingly, Uncle Aubrey connected even less when he returned to his home patch on his leaving of the army after five years; Aunt Annie with her fiery-red wavy hair was Ma's childhood buddy and confidante. She also had the sweet wrinkly eyes of a woman who could see no wrong in you yet would bark and frighten the living daylights out of her own offspring. This double personality worked wonders for getting one over our cousins as she was all too willing to see one of her own offspring as the 'guilty' party rather than the likes of me. Rubbing a cousin's nose in it usually took the form of a sly cheeky grin behind Aunt Annie's back; Aunt Silvia with her high-pitched and everlasting laugh was a joy to witness — but it was either this or the dagger-edged tongue of a woman who would give Queen Victoria a run for her money. Aunt Silvia's hysteria would certainly give the 'adult talking room' an air of light-heartedness yet she did nothing to defend red-headed people against the social stereotyping onslaught that patented them as short-fused and ill-tempered; finally, Uncle Ronnie with his sullen demeanour that rendered him an outcast by the rest of the family, in conversational terms. His withdrawal behind the hippy-length hair and masses of facial growth might have been hip for the times, but this coupled with a quirky silence only led to everyone else ignoring him to the point that he wasn't even seen in the same room as them.

Me extended family of Sherrards from Drumalief then, were constant, consistent and clearly recognisable — the Kennedys of Letterkenny, however, were a different matter. Da's ma and da were not alive for me to create any sense of bonding yet I longed to hear about them — the less that was said the more intriguing they became. Therefore, when Ma and Da talked one day about sorting out their grave in Letterkenny's Church of Ireland graveyard I jumped at the chance to be there.

# Chapter 4
## Ma and Da's Graveyard Trip

I didn't tell Ma and Da that I was interested in going to the graveyard — previous enthusiastic attempts to probe into Kennedy family history ended in frowns that spoke volumes of taboo and distaste. Da's frown indicated that his parents were not for me to know about, whilst Ma's frown was more about "don't dare to annoy your father".

Like any mystery, any version of the unknown, any sense of variation to the norm or any form of conspiracy, I was absolutely captivated. I think this is such a universal human trait — being curious or downright nosey! You only have to witness the queues of motorway traffic looking on at an accident that had taken place on the opposite side of the road, to see the manifestation of human curiosity at its peak.

In terms of Da's family, how best then, to stir the interest of a potential audience than to try to hide what they seek to view. Salman Rushdie, George Bernard Shaw and D.H. Lawrence surely know what I'm talking about — they may never have become who they did without the banning, secrecy and taboo-ing of their works. It goes to say too, that a good old scandal (especially when sex is present) also works as a phenomenal marketing tool; the classic *Lady Chatterley's Lover* and the more contemporary *Fifty Shades of Grey* trilogy are perfect examples of this theory, regardless of their literary quality.

I didn't tell me mates about the graveyard trip for fear of mocking and exclusion; there was always enough of a dosage of slagging to be had on any given day of the week at the best of times without giving me mates additional ammunition. Me lack of imaginative ideas couldn't conjure up a spellbinding story to tell them even though a graveyard theme had all the markings of spiritual beings and ghastly ghouls. I only hoped that I would be able to tell them something spectacular on me return and not be seen as just weird!

Of course, the 'graveyard shift' was on a Sunday — trips into Donegal were always on a Sunday (unless it was during the August holiday fortnight when weekday trips took place). Sundays were always uncannily depressing regardless if we went on a trip to relatives, to the beach or not. Of course, staying indoors in Alfred Street all day after the bleak sessions of Sunday school and church were without doubt much worse. The religiously Victorian ethos of keeping the Sabbath holy was Da's responsibility — holy meant not going outdoors for any form of recreation, and therefore not being open to ridicule by so-called God-fearing neighbours. No one who saw themselves as God-fearing folk wanted to be seen by others as blasphemous, so they hid inside the four walls of their houses content in the assumption that everyone respected their respecting of the Scriptures. What might really have gone on behind closed doors was never talked about. On a positive note, at least I didn't have to dream up some excuse to satisfy me mates in not playing with them as I never played with them on a Sunday anyway.

Da epitomised this cultural norm much to the frustration of all us kids. This dough of frustration rose into a gigantic loaf of hyperbolic crust when we could hear many a friend playing outside, as if Christ hadn't existed in the first place, never mind rising from the dead on the Sabbath. They obviously didn't come from a God-fearing house like me. I was definitely on their wavelength but Da and many other parents (Protestants) from the Four Streets weren't. There might have been a time when one of me older siblings had dared to ask to play outside but that double-dare must have happened well before my time because it just wasn't an option as far as I can recount. As far as I was concerned, Da and his 'brethren' were the nation of hypocrisy. Hypocrisy played a huge part in their lives and of many of those around me — a trait that I grew to detest, and still do, with a passion fit for any Pagan chieftain going into battle. At least going to me grandparents' grave was one up on being held prisoner in me own house — Hobson's got a lot to answer for!

So off to Letterkenny we went — Ma, Da, Paul,

Isobel and me. The others had special dispensation to stay at home on the grounds of being old enough to opt out of family trips. Opting to be stuck at home on a dull and boring Sunday was something I couldn't fathom; at least it meant there was space for us to move around in Da's beloved, maroon-coloured Wolseley. This was a brother version of the laid-to-rest Morris Oxford as far as I was concerned, as it looked virtually the same to me (except, of course, for its colour) with its pointed wings and array of shiny chrome. Oh, that chrome, that chrome that I could never polish as shiny to meet Da's unreachable standards.

As usual we left after the fantastic Sunday dinner, all three courses: starters (though we never used to call it anything) was home-made vegetable soup made with the stock of a chicken that had been boiled for hours in a huge metal pan the previous night while Cilla Black and the Black and White Minstrels burst their lungs on the black and white box; the main meal (we just called it dinner) was sliced carrots (rounded, of course), tinned peas, green cabbage, turnip (swede didn't exist in Irish vocabulary), boiled unskinned potatoes (gosh I hated taking time out to peel them on a side plate — and what a waste of vitamins!) and all watered down with runny, dark brown gravy. Yorkshire pudding wasn't served — it was something I never saw in Ireland and never eaten till I crossed the Irish Sea years later. I still find the variations of Sunday roasts depending on locale, amazing, and even more amazing that each person seems to fiercely defend their own style, voicing that theirs is the one true to tradition; finally, came pudding (not dessert) — runny custard to make sure there was enough to go around, covering some apple or rhubarb crumble (me favourite).

Why is it, a dinner cooked by someone else always tastes better than yours? Also, why is it that despite all the beautiful dinners since those halcyon days, I (and many others) always end up making comparisons, and in doing so, trying me utmost not to offend the cook who made it? I guess we all have our treasured recipes which bring out the bias in us based on nostalgia and innocence.

The three-course meal and the gathering of family around the table to eat it is something that has become extinct in many households through time; not everything about evolution is to be rejoiced. For years now I can just about manage two courses at a push — I wish I could say that it was due to a shrinking stomach but me trouser waist size rules that one out. As well as that, eating at the table is an infrequent event — the couch just takes over and pulls you unto it regardless of the willpower that struggles to fend it off. Confession — laziness! So, there's something about harking back to a tradition that no longer exists in me life and that I'm responsible for — a regret here. Wonder if I'll change?

Leaving for anywhere straight after the Sunday dinner never happened in our house, so departure for the grave trip was no different. Ma was responsible for the delays but no blame or finger-pointing could take place — after all, she was the one who made sure that all signs that a family dinner had taken place were no longer visible. I can say that now but at the time I was the typical impatient, inconsiderate, oblivious kid who expected to leave ten minutes after stuffing me face. Thirty minutes was an age, but two hours was a custodial sentence. Thankfully, *The Big Match* with Brian Moore was on UTV, showing highlights of Saturday's footy games. Watching me glorious Arsenal with their contingent of Irish players (me biased subconscious must have been on the throne when I was deciding which First Division team to support) and fantasising about copying the swinging hips and slalom running of Georgie Best (not an Arsenal player) en route to scoring a screamer, helped for the first hour of waiting for Ma. Funny that the iconic status of Georgie Best wasn't enough to entice me into hanging on to his shirt tail and to follow the red of Manchester United like many of me mates.

The second hour was sheer torment as Ma was upstairs out of sight getting herself ready (whatever that meant) and the telly was then taken over by the bullying older sisters Val, Hazel and Irene who claimed ownership of the channel to be watched — usually, in me own biased eyes, some old, boring romantic film with Cary Grant on BBC2. Me and Paul couldn't face such soppy stuff and went off to the 'unused' sitting room to get rid of the dreaded homework, but only after procrastinating for the first ten minutes of the film in the vague hope that it might be watchable — motivation for doing homework was not a gift we possessed.

Ma appeared about three o'clock dressed in her Sunday best — chequered, tricolour, knee-length woollen skirt, olive polo-neck cotton top and thick Arran cardigan (a coat was rarely an option), tan-coloured stockings and slip-on brown, patent, low-heeled shoes with their customary imitation gold square buckle. Her image wasn't anything too fancy or striking, and as visiting family or the odd acquaintance only happened once or twice a month, then who would notice if the same garments were worn each time or not? I just couldn't get to grips with the length of time it took her to change, brush her hair and dab on a bit of make-up!

Of course, Ma's appearance meant we were leaving. However, mine and Paul's initial enthusiasm to escape the droning den of boredom had by this stage faded considerably so we couldn't greet her arrival with any sense of joy, or relief. Da, on the other hand, had dozed off as per usual and jumped to attention as if rudely awoken by the sergeant major whilst on night duty — after all, Ma standing with handbag on forearm and arms folded always told him that a state of urgency was demanded. He never liked to displease her about anything; in fact, she was the only one he would submit to about anything. Those moments of submission were awesome for us to witness, it was like watching the great wolf pack leader cow down and trundle off with

43

his tail between his legs. I think some transference of his own ma was clearly evident as Ma rarely had to say anything to him or even frown. Wow, to have such power!

So, into the Wolseley the four of us got. Isobel was left behind as at the eleventh hour it was deemed inappropriate to bring a two-year-old to a graveyard — brill, more space in the back seat and no whinging or crying or being a pain to put up with. It was rare that me and Paul had the back seat all to ourselves — our enthusiasm was re-ignited.

The journey was a rough one as the Free State roads were never as smooth as those in the North. The roads came in two types: the narrow, crater-dotted one with more unevenness than a muddy cows' field, and the newly surfaced one with an inch of loose stones that pelted the underside of the car. The former tested the digesting of the earlier Sunday dinner and assessed if vertigo was at large, whilst the latter brought on a temporary hearing impairment. Familiarity with these roads encouraged me to look out for any signs of road surface progress since we were last on them — sadly there never was. Ten years later the same roadwork signs, the same 'European Funding Development' signs and the same constantly displaced loose stones were evident — any optimism and hope of road evolution I previously had, had died the death years before then.

Like many small towns in Ireland, Letterkenny could be seen from a few miles out as it was situated on top of a small hill and had the Church of Ireland church spire reaching higher towards its parishioners' heaven than any other building or structure. It was not infrequent to see the battle of the spires take place in many an Irish town in Donegal or in the North of Ireland — one representing the Protestant Church of Ireland and one representing a saint-named Catholic chapel. I'm not sure if the architects were responsible for this fight for God's affections, or the religious leaders, or whether it was just an attribute of chance. Yes, I think I'll opt for the pagan-inspired argument.

The wrought-iron gates greeted us with the solemnity fitting for the entrance to a graveyard with its bleak, black and barren setting. Me original enthusiasm for the trip (somewhat dampened by the journey as Da drove slower than normal so he could reminisce) returned instantly at the sight of such a threshold — though thoughts of spooky things brought me out in goosebumps. No one said anything either which reflected some tension in Ma and Da, whilst it also added to the eeriness all around us. Da got from the boot the spade, bucket, shears (borrowed from a work colleague as we had nothing green to dig or cut in our concrete backyard), and a handful of huge paper bags, that once housed purdies. He then led the way up the steep, weed-covered gravel path to the unknown, without saying anything or even looking at Ma. He always liked to lead the way like a 'civilised' apache scout who had left his roots behind and joined up with the uniformed 'white man', and who constantly kept a twenty-yard distance between himself and the less able posse behind him. Normally this wouldn't bother me or Paul, but on this occasion the inner energy of fear and anticipation drove us to stay close behind him — after all, he had the weapons to see off any nasty ghosts or ghouls whose 'holy ground' we were trespassing. The thought of spooky creatures always made me chest rise and fall in that awful slow and almost frozen-like rhythm, whether it be in me bedroom or looking out over the Tins at night, but entering their own backyard made me whole frame tense up whilst me eyes felt as big as me head. Me ears were as alert as a bat's. It was amazing how me senses suddenly became more acute, I could see detail of me surrounding so vividly whilst I could hear absolutely anything around me; from a dead and withered leaf weaving its way through the willow tree on the way to the ground, to the flapping fan-shaped wings of a raven flying homeward before the fall of darkness.

Looking behind me I could see Ma calmly struggling up the hill. How come she didn't seem bothered? She obviously wasn't on the same macho mission as us, so it was just me, Paul and Da. The aliens' territory seemed to get darker too, the nearer we got to the old creepy church at the top. Captain Kirk was always being faced with this kind of hostile atmosphere and enemy terrain but he could be beamed up if he was in bother — we didn't have a Scottie to transport us back to the warm and safe Enterprise! Nothing around really sunk in till we reached the levelling at the church's entrance. Pausing for breath I began to look around: disjointed rows of immovable stone headstones and crosses of different shapes, sizes, forms stared back at me at various angles amongst the foot-long wet, green grass. Which one were we looking for? Would we have to walk across other graves to get to the one we were searching for? Just as me imagination was about to explode, I heard the heavy sound of boots emerging from the back of the church.

"How ye doin'? What can I do fir ye?" The voice was husky and soft, and clearly that of a local man. The whole graveyard seemed to lighten up as if the spirits had run back into their hidey-holes. This man was me saviour — we had won. It was just as well I'd heard his dusty tones prior to seeing his face as his bluish-red leathery skin, moth-bitten clown nose and slanted eyes peering from beneath an unwashed cloth cap would have convinced me that he was indeed the keeper of the graveyard's spirits rather than keeper of the graves.

After we let Da exchange words with this man and delve into his Letterkenny accent and dialect with a sense of ease and nostalgia, we were escorted to a patch of unkempt grass that lay amongst a mixture of similar patches and other clearly marked graves with huge stone crosses or finely chiselled and polished headstones. Was this it? Was this why we had made this expedition for, a patch of long grass? Paul looked at me and our thoughts were mirrored. Any idea of digging or cutting grass was repulsed by both of us simultaneously and quickly replaced by thoughts of doing some apache scouting whilst in enemy territory. This was new land to explore, no need to pretend that Commanche or Navajo braves were nearby and ready to ambush our war party, like we would normally do whilst in the familiar turf of the Tins; this was adrenalin-pumping and life-threatening stuff.

Da had no intentions of letting us tamper with the grave of his own ma and da, so we quickly scarpered before being told to stay in the one spot where we could be seen. Da was always the 'expert' and only he could sort the grave properly which typically reflected all manual jobs performed at home; he never let us do anything with any tool, whether it be hammer, screwdriver or paintbrush. We could never do it properly or at a satisfactory speed — so we became the unskilled workforce. Not surprisingly, DIY as a homeowner in later life was a painful learning curve. Not only did I have to learn from a continuum of errors but I constantly had to fight the dreaded voice in me head telling me that I couldn't do it in the first place and only failure waited to witness me downfall. Needless to say, procrastinating with DIY jobs is something I still do regularly, whilst despite the numerous achievements in this field I still feel like that incompetent eight-year-old boy. I know I won't change regardless of the building feats accomplished and the heaps of admiration from others. I can feel self-pride being allowed in to visit more than in the past and that without question is a lovely feeling, but it certainly doesn't lead to any shouting from the rooftops.

After seeing off ten thousand strong Indian braves (Da was too busy working to ensure we stayed in the same spot), me and Paul returned to the rectangular plot of land. Our return wasn't so much to see the result of Da's Protestant work ethic (though the grave did look neat and would be greater improved when the ordered headstone was fixed in a few weeks' time), but more because darkness had beaten off the murky sunlight and fear of awakening ghosts was too unbearable. Being next to Da and Ma and the old man felt a few degrees safer if only because they didn't seem bothered at all about the lack of light or concerned about where we actually were. Sharing our fear with them would have been futile as we would have been unheard and it probably would have resulted in being told off for having such feelings in the first place, never mind for declaring them!

Parents never seemed to take time out to listen, so it became customary to keep such things to meself. How did today's generation of parents get to the stage of listening to their offspring anyway? Somebody must have started the ball rolling? I don't remember there being a government advertising campaign promoting parents to give their children attention and to practise their listening skills. Also, where did that parent and child relationship-building phrase 'quality time' come from? Another one of those mysteries of evolution that would later appear in 'Best Parenting' books I suppose. It's funny that such forms of teaching appeared in books long after they were in evidence in actual mainstream parenting curricula. Even more ironic would be the fact that an author of one of these books would make it sound as if they were creating their own form of scripture for us mere parent readers to worship. On the other hand, fair play to them for making money out of telling us what we had already been doing!

By the time we got back into the car the whole graveyard was so black that the ghosts would have had to have been white to be seen. Nevertheless, even the safe haven of the back seat of the Wolseley wasn't enough to settle me breathing or calm me nerves or to stop me bulging eyes from straining out of the window for any flicker of life or death. We'd only been at this deadly place for about half an hour, but it seemed like ages. I'd had a big enough dose of darkness. Thankfully, before me imagination got going again, Ma's pangs of guilt of not seeing Da's family and relatives then took over, so a trip to some of his few living relatives in Manorcunningham on the way back was planned.

The Steeles of Manorcunningham were one of two of Da's remaining families who lived not far from Letterkenny (the other was the Stewarts). These two groups were Da's remaining closest relatives; the others were mere cousins living in Derry itself. Just as the death of Da's sisters was a taboo subject and kept to extreme levels of confidentiality, so was the exact details and connections of these 'distant' relatives. Listening to adult conversation was something I didn't do at the best of times, so it was by pure chance that I sewed a few patches of information together and created a family quilt that showed Da was the nephew of Emily Steele from Manorcunningham and also of Robert George Stewart, Stanley Stewart (never referred to as uncles) and Aunt Mary Jane Stewart from 'down the steep lane' — their farm was never given a name. Any time we ventured in the direction of Letterkenny we would alternate visits to one of these houses that seemed frozen in an era and in an environment so different to the 'urban' ghetto of the Four Streets in Derry.

Both families were farmers — the Steeles were prospering cattle farmers and the Stewarts were those who farmed a mixture of livestock. Both families and their homes were so far removed from me existence in Derry that they were more on par with the Ulster Folk Museum I visited in primary school. In fact, those school trips were deemed to be about learning of how people used to live and would create joyous excitement on the bus journey there. But as me mates would utter noises of wonderment at 'ancient' farming tools, peat slowly burning in a stone fireplace and the smells of home-made bread emanating from the rustic-built cottage kitchen, I was left with me thoughtful words "it's no big deal". There was no way I'd tell the others of me boredom or the reason for that as they would either be jealous or not believe me; either way I'd be slagged relentlessly for weeks.

The Steeles' home was a bungalow/one-storey cottage sandwiched between other similar bungalows that faced a replica line of dwellings on the other side of the wide main street. The width of such a road was not in line with such a sleepy, ghost-town-of-a-village, with only about sixty dwellings in total. Why was the road so wide? Like many others questions I didn't ask adults this one — and guessed in later years that noisy agricultural traffic and herded livestock might have had something to do with it. Cars were few and far between too and those that were there didn't look fit to pass any level of MOT — the layer of mud that clung to the layers of rust seemed to somehow keep them in one piece. The road was bordered by a foot-high kerb that made a clear dividing line between what people walked on and what the passing herd of cattle stomped on. Stepping on the eighteen-inch-wide flat kerb was out of bounds in Da's rule book. Only a silly moment of daring would allow any of us kids to step on it for fear of Da's X-ray eyes that could see through walls catching us. There wasn't much we could do on the pavement to keep us entertained — even the luxury of footy with a tennis ball was out of the question. We couldn't make much noise either as we'd be called inside. The fact that it was usually a Sunday when we called to this remote place meant that Sunday rules of 'children shall not be heard' had to be honoured. It was clearly less boring being outside than inside. What was always distinctive was the smell of cows and what they projected from their digestive system — even if there wasn't any actual cow dung in the street. Mixed with the smell of burning peat, the air was potent to say the least — but it was different to what we were used to and therefore had that typical nostalgic feel about it. Darkness would inevitably fall and do what it did best — round up all kids off the streets and into the safety of their houses.

So on this occasion, as there weren't any big sisters to act as the messenger, Da came out to fetch us in. If it had been Val or Hazel, we could have stalled for a further five minutes, but as it was Da, going inside was immediate. We perched ourselves at the table at the back of the large square room as the adults were gathered on battered old armchairs around the glowing fire. Being now dark meant that the back window was obliterated by the dirty, gold-coloured thick curtains. Saying that, even in the brightness of summer's evening you couldn't see out of the filthy window anyway so I never knew what existed outside the window. It was tempting to have a peek behind the curtains but neither of us would dare to touch them in case we'd be caught. Doing forbidden things in your own house was bad enough, and which would often bring on Da's infamous Celtic cry "What 'r' ye at?" that was pronounced as one word and rose in pitch towards the end, but 'sinning' in someone else's house brought on a severe whack on the arm or body or leg or whatever body part Da could reach as he'd spring from his chair like a cat who'd been waiting patiently for his moment to strike on its vulnerable prey. You'd never see it coming so the element of surprise always had its full impact. I suppose there was always that naïve notion that I might get away with whatever it was I might get away with. I lived in hope, but that was a hope built without foundation, favourable historical data or recent experience. I would never make an Errol Flynn or a John Wayne who seemed to effortlessly outwit their enemies without any hint of rehearsing or planning. How do you make yourself out to be cleverer? I'd often think that the answer didn't lie in books or some random sage, but in some natural phenomena or muse that would come to me or develop in me one day. This was something I knew I couldn't force or conjure up; I'd have to be patient and wait for it to happen — I was in me teens before it did to some extent.

So the back of the Steeles' house was never discovered. What was visible was what was inside. There was the stone-paved flooring without any sign of rug or mat that echoed the hobnail boots that frequently paced over it. Heating was a problem anyway but the freezing floor only exacerbated the coldness that blew in from the icy waters of the Atlantic and gathered momentum as it forced its way over Lough Swilly, and found its way through the frequently opened, latched wooden door.

Nevertheless, there were greater revelations that captivated me on every trip we made there: one was the use of 'farming currency' and the other was the Irish television channel RTE where Irish Gaelic was the only language spoken.

It seemed like something out of the Dark Ages to see locals enter the cottage from the darkness, dressed in dark clothes regardless of the season — only the numbers of layers of clothing changed depending on the time of year. Emily and George Steele would greet them on first name terms. They'd come in for a slab of butter to be wrapped in greaseproof paper or have their tin jug filled with fresh cows' milk. Why didn't they go to a shop, I'd think — it seemed such a cheek to invade someone's privacy at any time of day or night by knocking at the door, letting themselves in and all for something as basic as milk or butter. It seemed even more antisocial to do it on a 'holy' Sabbath and when visitors were present. Why didn't these people stock up the day before? Having an 'open' door may have been a typical cultural trait across the British Isles during decades of the twentieth century but I can empathise with its decline and a move towards locked doors and a more 'this is my space' psyche.

These 'invaders' would often throw a coin or two into a tin bowl that lay on the big table at the other end of the room, on the way out, and this was obvious payment. The coins, however, were alien to me as they had Irish words written on them and different, unrecognisable faces imprinted on one side — the Queen's head was nowhere to be seen. I had the same feelings of curiosity and intrigue years later when me sister Irene would arrive back from Germany or Brazil, or me sister Hazel from Spain, both with their foreign coins of pirate booty. Their loose change from times abroad never seemed real, but that you would play a board game with, and when we used it during our fantasy games of playing shop or post office there would be a degree of flippancy and excited extravagance when spending it. Nevertheless, there was something different about these coins thrown into the tin bowl — they were counted in punts, Irish pounds. Now I used pounds and Ma and Da used pounds but they weren't given any nationality — years later 'our' coins were described to me as English pounds but that didn't help the situation — why not British pounds? So pounds across the border in the Free State were different, but as usual it was never explained, so that was something else to work out for meself. Looking back, I wish I'd kept a list of 'unexplained' things and written a book entitled 'Everything You Wanted To Know As A Child, But Was Unexplained: The Answers' — maybe that'll be a future challenge.

The Irish coins were one thing to get me head round but when coins weren't exchanged for the dairy produce then it was slices of ham, pork chops of various sizes, rashers of bacon or even balls of wool. The same words of "thankin' you now" were ushered regardless of the currency. This truly was symbolic of a world beyond the one I was familiar with in Derry. Everybody seemed happy with the arrangement and although I couldn't fathom how the Steeles could spend or use all the payment they received I was content with their contentment.

If the 'swap shop' grabbed me and Paul's curiosity then the Irish spoken on the telly and the frenetic Gaelic games of football and hurling made the times tables competition or the spelling tests, which captivated us in school, seem like Third Division stuff. Being of Protestant stock I was alien to anything *really* 'Irish' — whether it was sport, music, dancing, language or ideology (the latter mainly involved freedom from the English). So, what I saw and heard on the Steeles' RTE channel was strange yet thrilling. Normally, we'd be at the Steeles' during either the news or sport programmes, or both. Even the news was captivating, as I'd try and decipher what was being said (even Da would leave his OCD ritual of watching every news bulletin behind in Derry for these visits). Although I didn't know it at the time, this was me primary introduction to the complex planet of linguistics. In me innocence and complete ignorance, I observed syntax, semantics, tone, rhetoric, rhythm and any vowel or consonant sounds that echoed those I knew in English — all in me vain attempt to grasp any meaning being conveyed by the newsreader. Occasionally, there would be the typical black and white recorded footage of a story accompanied by the newsreader's guttural and phlegmatic voice-over. Me and Paul would have great fun at creating our own voice-overs. A picture of two smartly dressed politicians in suits shaking hands and smiling would have the voice-over of:

"And the two eejits from the North and South Poles were told by their mammies to stop their fightin' over a block of ice and to show the world that they were friends. The whites of their knuckles when they shook hands for the first time and their big cheesy grins proved they were only pretendin' in order to dodge having their legs smacked. But their mammies were happy."

There was certainly immense fun to be had during what would otherwise be a tortuous hour or so of sheer boredom. It was really hard to stifle the giggles as me comments and Paul's comments would get more ridiculous, more absurd and funnier as we practised. We would feed off each other so well and work in perfect comic tandem that it was not surprising we were always spoken of in stigmatic double-act terms as 'the boys' or 'the twins' or 'two peas in a pod'. The latter certainly had villainous overtones, with only some occasions warranting such a tag. It was only a matter of time then that our exuberance would push Da's patience over the edge (the edge was never far away from our point of view anyway) and we'd have the usual public humiliation of a slap. The slap always stung to the bone but with tears in our eyes we'd have to avoid eye contact to avoid setting each other off on another fit of stifled giggles — we would then be at the mercy of the other elders' supportive comments to prevent a second cuff.

The Gaelic sports on the Irish television channel, on the other hand, created a thrill amongst the graveyard conversation of adults — literal on this visit, but the topic of conversation never seemed to stretch much beyond all things 'grave'. Being keen sporty lads, me and Paul would have been over the moon if darts or snooker or even show jumping came on the telly, but the all-action, fast-paced and physical brutality of Gaelic football and hurling was pure bliss. I would have loved to have played these games in school, but Protestant 'siege' mentality (based on the notion of defending British Northern Ireland from the so-called Catholic Irish enemy including anything remotely Irish) and Catholic-'oppressed' mentality (based on keeping out anything remotely British in nature including Protestantism) meant I was never given that opportunity. Such restrictions are present around the globe, I'm sure, but to a young eight-year-old, the baffling circus of politics was out of rational reach and only served to heighten the flummoxing dichotomy of a Protestant way of life and a Catholic one — unfortunately I still find meself trying to explain the unexplainable to someone outside this environment. Frustration.

So watching Kerry or Sligo or Dublin competing against any one of me own counties from Ulster, in front of screaming thousands at Croke Park had me and Paul completely entranced. Fierce competition was something we could definitely relate to, but to see men batter each other in tackle (legitimate or otherwise), run like weaving comic figures when chased by hungry hounds with hurling sticks and show flashes of dazzling skill to score points and goals made the boring trip to Donegal relatives all worthwhile — well, nearly. The excited and high-speed commentary in a language I couldn't comprehend didn't spoil the fun — in fact, I would silently create me own commentary. Commentating is something I've developed over the years having first practised on muddy patches of wasteland over the Tins when scoring goals between the jumper goalposts, and in later years shouting at the action on Sky Sports. I've always had a childlike dream of being a football commentator on the television and even now drive me family up the walls by having me comments echoed by those well-paid pundits and commentators on the box. We can carve out many of our paths in our life's journey with determination, willpower, grit and skillset, but sometimes certain paths are beyond our reach because getting on to them is just about who you know or if 'your face fits'. It then takes courage and resilience to move on from such a barrier (and probable disappointment) and focus on what control we *do* have. One vocation lost.

The visit at the Steeles' came to an end in the way most visits there did, with Da standing up, putting his coat on, crudely ushering us boys out of our TV gaze regardless of whether the action had finished or not, and then more feebly asking Ma if she was ready to go. I knew that I wouldn't get the chance to watch the beloved Gaelic games again for some time and left wishing we lived on the west side of the River Foyle in Derry and not the east side. Those on the Catholic-dominated west side were able to receive the RTE transmitter. How was I ever to embrace a sense of Irishness if I couldn't even watch the Irish telly channel? Like a lot of things as a child, I would have to take a proactive role, and like a lot of things this would have to wait till I was older and more confident to break away from the 'British' culture that surrounded me. I would have to be patient.

The remaining journey from Manorcunningham to Derry was again typical of many journeys in the darkness of night which involved crossing over the border from the 'South' to the 'North' during the Troubles.

Bombs going off in the distance, the consequent smoke signals that rivalled any created by the brave Apache, peppered gunfire, noisy police sirens, army foot patrols who sauntered no less so on the tarmac Irish streets as they would have done in the swamp undergrowth of Vietnam, and breeze block corrugated army checkpoints on the Irish/British border were commonplace. Funnily, all this didn't really make me feel necessarily scared — it was more a case of intrigue, nervous excitement and confusion. Fear though was in the air, and I breathed it in like everyone else during the Troubles. It's funny to return to Derry and love the cooler and fresher air that I breathe in, but it still contains fear. I'm definitely more aware of this fear when I return now, but that's probably because I'm less immune to it now as it doesn't spit its daily venom in the way it once did when I lived there.

Yet Ma's constant worried tones, gasping exclamations and constant fidgeting on the passenger seat as we approached the Letterkenny Road border checkpoint was enough to create wobbles in the most secure and stable of children. It's amazing how panic can easily set in. Ma's injection of trepidation swept across me body entering every bone, nerve and muscle till I was utterly stiff with tension. Goosebumps sprouted all over me before attempting to jump out of me skin with their own fear of dying whilst helplessly still attached to me. On the last furlong of this graveyard trip, she got herself going as usual by uttering, "Hope there's not trouble tonight!" It was if she was psyching herself up for the worst so she could avoid any possible sudden shock, as this would be too much for her to bear. Why didn't she just keep her qualms to herself? Surely, she had a responsibility to us kids? There would be times when thinking aloud was harmless ("Shall I cook liver or sausages for tea?") or produced only a few ripples ("I'm sure it was cancer that killed him"), but this was not the place. It only took an oncoming car's headlights flashing (warning drivers that there was something serious involving the army or police up ahead) or the sound of an army helicopter high in the dark sky, or a faint ambulance siren, or the toxic smell of smoke seeping through the car's ventilators to get her going. In fact, Ma new all the danger signs and finely tuned all her senses to tap into them. Saying that, I can't remember a journey home from the Free State when there wasn't some 'sign' that the Troubles was uttering something from its poisoned gaping mouth. On this occasion it was the long queue of traffic that announced itself by the twisting red curves of tail lights ahead of us. "Oh gosh" was the cry as always and I knew then that her fears were realised and that we were to have some awkward, dodgy or tense moments ahead of us.

Da as usual couldn't understand what Ma was fussing about — in fact, they became polarised in their responses as Da loved any sense of trouble, danger or conflict and therefore thrived on the things that drove Ma to the realms of panic. His juxtaposed calmness (not often visible, but there) certainly helped counter Ma's increasing flustering. I knew that its temporal effect would soon be realised, as he would drive into the focal point of any fracas in order to witness at first hand, or as near as damn it, whatever it was. I'm sure he'd have made a fantastic BBC correspondent in any war-torn country — he certainly practised often enough in front of us in our kitchen!

He would undoubtedly push Ma's boundaries and patience to the limit on such occasions, which ended in her explosive command:

"You'll do no such thing!"

Her face would be tense, her eyes would be bulging and her jawbone would be rigid. Silence would follow until Da navigated a wider girth around the most recent flare-up that played outside in the Derry air. Chit-chat would start up but only of a reflective and inquisitive nature. Ma would move on and forget about the whole issue, but Da's obsessive compulsion to find out the exact details of the whole event via the radio or telly on arrival home never allowed him such refuge — or us either.

On this occasion, there was no avoiding the army checkpoint ahead — in fact, any U-turning on the Letterkenny Road would be spotted by the helicopter overhead and we'd be instantly identified as potential terrorists. Da knew his teasing limits by not even attempting to suggest that one to Ma. So there we were, stuck in this long line of every car model you could think of — Escort, Maxi, Mini, Austin 1100, Beetle and Morris Minor, would definitely be there. All I could see were red dots of the tail lights, alternating between dim and shining bright, depending on whether the brake pedal was being pushed to the floor of the car or not, or whether the handbrake was lifted or not. I became fixated at watching this procession of varied redness and as the furthest car's set of lights got dimmer, I'd anticipate the domino effect take place as all the lights of all the cars behind it would get dimmer too — one by one, till it was Da's turn to release his handbrake and we'd move forward a few feet. I'd keep one eye though on the cars up ahead to make sure I saw the front car's lights turn brighter again and the opposite would happen. I longed for Da to lift his handbrake before the front car's lights changed, but they never did; the snake moved ever so slowly.

As the snake got shorter, we got nearer.

There it is, I whispered to meself — 'Colditz'. As the small red security torch of an army officer (well, the front man always had some white stripes on his uniform) flashed through the blackened sky as it told each car to veer to the left or to the right, I could make out the fortress all around us. The lookout towers were dotted around in a square shape. Their pointed, corrugated tin heads and long cold, legless bodies stood strong and powerful against the blowing rain that had suddenly appeared as it always did in Ireland, from nowhere. The small gap between the head and body housed the soldiers with their automatic machine guns and huge circular light that only came on when there was a sense of 'enemy' presence. I knew the soldiers were there with their blackened faces and camouflage combat gear — I couldn't see them now but I could in daylight. It was all right in the daytime when I could picture them as young men with their favourite football team's shirt on or having fish and chips around the tea table with their wife and children. Now though, they were menacing, sneaky and hostile — they were the evil

Germans or Vietcong waiting for an excuse to exterminate us. It was difficult at that time to see them as the evil British as they were the ones I admired and 'fought' with in all the war films. I know many people did see the British as the enemy but it was years later before I understood why.

Huge walls of dark green, corrugated sheets were everywhere — we were trapped in their compound and we couldn't leave till they said so. Worse to come was the concrete block walls of the compound's gut. Here the blinding security lights set alight its central organs — the main post in the middle of the road where the tip of a rifle poked out (at least it didn't have the round laser knob at the end of it like the daleks did or I really would have been scared). This housed some hi-tech equipment that checked car registration details and driver's licence details — how could they know all about all of us, I'd think. And then make a judgement that you were worth letting go, worth bringing you 'in' for further checks or simply a 'terrorist'. High walls to the left and right segregated the cars that were having a more thorough checking.

Cows and sheep at the local Lisahally market outside of Derry must have had similar treatment — straight ahead if succulent beef within, left if underweight, and right if more fit for hamburgers and pies. I wonder what each one might have thought as they approached the cloth-capped, red-faced chief of the market:

"Oh yes, I'm so good, straight ahead I go!"

"The snobby bitch, she never gave the rest of us a chance, with the way she gobbled up the grass!"

"Oh shite!"

There were nights when we were merely waved on by the small red dot in the air without Da even winding his window down. He always looked rejected and dejected when that happened and would move off in a straight line with a grunt. Ma would just stare straight ahead whilst holding her breath, too frightened to utter any sound for fear of bringing some unwanted attention from the soldiers — she just wanted to get as far away as possible from the checkpoint, and as far away as possible from potential gunfire or bombs! Shootings and bombings *did* happen every once in a while at a checkpoint. We *did* get caught up in a shop bombing once, but more of that later.

In terms of getting pulled over to the right for further interrogation, that only happened on one occasion and that was when we'd been returning, via a detour to avoid rioting in Strabane, on the way back from Dublin.

The car was jam-packed with Irene's (second eldest in family) student stuff and a soldier had spotted a book about Irish history on the back shelf with the Irish flag of green, white and gold on the front cover. Of course, flags and colours are highly symbolic all over the world, but in Ireland symbolism takes on hyperbolically stereotypical proportions. Red or blue means you're a

British-thinking Orangeman who hates all Catholics, all things papal and all things Irish, whilst green and yellow (substitute for gold) means that you're an Irish freedom fighter who hates the English, the British and every Protestant who dares utter the name Ian Paisley — and, of course, a potential terrorist and member of, or prospective member of, the IRA. It goes without saying that the perceived significance of such colour symbolism usually involved all of its potential interpretations, not one in isolation. So you couldn't be an Orangeman and see yourself as Irish or be anti-English and love Ian Paisley. This meant that in this situation we were seen by this particular British soldier as an extreme threat to his life and those he was on duty with. The saying, 'Better safe than sorry' is probably one of those ingrained and instinctive survival philosophies that kicks in when life is continually under threat — this guy was no different to the rest of us in such times. In fact, I've carried this way of thinking throughout me life — does that mean I've got a 'siege mentality' like many of me compatriots? Probably.

Well, true to form, the soldier ushered us to the right. Suddenly, the car was cut off from all other cars trying to get through the checkpoint — we were at the mercy of what seemed a whole platoon of British soldiers staring at us. I'd seen many soldiers before this on the streets of Derry, but this was different. Before, I was just a kid who was purely an enthusiastic observer of what they were doing — now we were the 'enemy'.

The painful silence in the car as a baby-faced soldier walked off with Da's driving licence was worse than any sound by Ma or Da could possibly be. Da had been ordered to switch the engine off so all I could hear was the occasional sound of another car having been given the all-clear and speeding off with puffs of relief blowing out from the exhaust and screams of euphoria coming from its engine. We were going nowhere.

I didn't know where to look, and I guess so did no one else. I counted ten unmoving, uniformed squaddies who looked more like cardboard cut-outs, with rifles placed diagonally across their stomachs and therefore with the ends pointed to the ground. I knew there were others out of sight but ready to take a pop if required. The war films on telly always had the likes of Clint Eastwood or Robert Mitchum with their men out in the open or at least within view of the camera lens, but they would have already given hand signals to less famous actors like Telly Savalas or Rob Steiger with their men, to be out of view of the Germans or Japs or whoever the foe was. The enemy were always fooled into thinking the opposition were under strength and therefore drawn into a false sense of security — I wasn't fooled.

I took it upon meself to be the unsung hero and therefore used me eyes to scour the hostile area for the other troops. If we knew where they were then we would be less likely to make a gesture or movement that might be deemed intimidating or threatening. I could speculate the tensions surrounding the soldiers and sense their overwhelming nervousness starting from the heart and making its way to the finger that ever-so-lightly caressed the trigger. One twitchy move or dodgy sound could set off the ammunition begging for their freedom (the shooting spree of Bloody Sunday was yet at its embryonic stage). By the time the soldier returned with Da's licence I had failed to spot any. I had to abort me mission.

"Excuse me, sir, I'd like you and all of your family to vacate the vehicle." His voice was neither harsh nor authoritative, yet no one was going to disobey him. His accent was what I'd come to believe was how all the English spoke; a kind of nondescript southern accent. It was a shock, a revelation and a delight to find out in later years the fantastic and colourful range of accents that were actually in existence across the Irish Sea. I should have had a better idea as I was very aware of the different accents that were divided by the River Foyle in Derry, never mind the vast differences between what could be heard in the main street in Strabane that lay to the south of Derry, with the speed and rhythm akin to inhabitants of Donegal, to that heard in the main street in Coleraine that lay to the north of Derry, where the intonation and vowel sounds were akin to the outer regions of Scotland's west coast.

The khaki-dressed defendant of the Queen's realm then guided us to a bench and asked us to remain calm, told us that this was just a routine check and therefore there was nothing to worry about. No words comforted

Ma as she gripped hold of toddler Isobel in her arms. Her face was drained of colour — for a redhead with constant rosy cheeks this was a feat she wasn't proud of. Irene was never good in any crisis and looked both puzzled and vacant. Paul, like me, was fascinated and a little scared — but working hard not to show it. Da had been accompanied into the breeze-block building to be asked questions about who we were, where we had come from and where we were going. Knowing Da, he was probably unfazed by everything. For a man who exploded at me or Paul for picking our noses or talking when the news was on the radio or telly, he became a colossus of calm in a real catastrophe. The one flaw in these moments where he survived with spirit and mind intact, was that he was hopeless in comforting others or showing any molecule of empathy or understanding. It was in this state that he walked back to us and glanced at the car's contents strewn all over the damp concrete ground — eerily there was barely a flicker of emotion. This merely acted as stark contrast to the rest of us who were in various degrees of distress. Ma was just about pipping Irene as Panic Queen.

Da then mechanically and methodically, whilst oozing composure, despite the interrogation, picked up our gear and placed it in the boot — Paul Daniels would have been proud of such a work of magic. It seemed miraculous that everything fitted — even though it had done so before we'd left Dublin five hours earlier. It's not that I think a woman can't load a car full of stuff neatly and systematically, but I've only ever seen a man do it — and what's more, me experience tells me that a woman tends to want the man or wait for the man to do it — another one of those subconscious-generated divisions of labour things.

Me and Paul didn't know who to watch — the soldiers with their camouflage gear and guns keeping a close eye on Da and us, Da packing the car or Ma and Irene rehearsing for a still life session at the local adult art class. I eventually decided that rotation was the best thing to do, so that I could keep tabs on all happenings. Out of boredom though, I found meself commentating like Brian Moore on UTV's *The Big Match*:

"He picks up the red record player with such ease and grace that he allowed himself space to turn towards the car without a hint of a soldier getting anywhere near him. He could turn on a sixpence, that lad. He shows much promise in this, his debut game, at Checkpoint Road in front of a capacity crowd. He's certainly one for the future.

"Goodness gracious me, Ma and Irene are rooted to the spot by that unbelievable bit of skill. It's almost as if they're stuck in the rain-soaked-ploughed field that always happens on this ground at this time of the year. It's such an advantage to the home side. In fact, their pale faces have 'shock' written all over them.

"And there goes the final whistle as the boot is finally slammed closed and once again the home guard go home with something to cheer about, though some of them still look in sombre mood draped in their black and green regalia. It was not the most entertaining of games but it was swathed in high drama and encapsulating tension."

It seemed an anti-climax to get back into the car and wave the soldiers goodbye. I was lost in me thoughts whilst Da went through his second interrogation for the day — this time under the auspices of Ma. In their dreamy voices expressing themselves outside of the action replays inside of me head, I could just about make out Ma's curiosity juxtaposed with her dread of the detail, whilst Da was well and truly the FA Cup-winning captain wallowing in glory and oracle-like status.

On this 'graveyard' checkpoint occasion, though, there was no such drama — straight on spoke the red torchlight. Da gave his customary one finger wave with his right hand as it rested on top of the steering wheel.

"It's the Donegal wave," he would call it. It's amazing how a single finger can transport such human contact and communication. It wasn't until I was much older and practising the art of the wave meself (especially in Ireland) that the true significance of the finger registered. At least I can say that I'm carrying on one traditional language steeped in cultural values — I only hope that me own offspring have been suitably indoctrinated to do the same.

The finger wave was given, but without its customary authenticity, probably because we weren't pulled over and he'd been disappointed. Da was never any good at pretending — whether it involved a negative or a positive emotion. Whatever his feeling or mood, you saw it on his sleeve, his face and heard it spat from his mouth. Ma, on the other hand, deserved Oscar-winning plaudits for some of her diplomacy and tact that hid real feelings of frustration, anger and disgust. It wasn't until she was in the security of her own family and far removed from the incident concerned that she felt free to let rip and condemn the guilty culprits to forty lashings from her tongue. Like all suppressed emotional upheavals of gigantic proportions, the outpouring of venom would be double the original feeling when it was given the freedom to live. So Da taught me to be true to meself at all times, whilst Ma taught me to be less congruent if confrontation was to be avoided. I think I swallowed Ma's pill for thirty-five years and found the build-up of unexpressed emotion a weight too much to bear, so I opened Da's treasure chest of free expression and spoke as I found — it's so therapeutic to let it all out when the need arises and let someone know when they've pissed me off. I must add though that this emotional cleansing does have a few grains of rationale and reasoning at times in order to avoid being seen as akin to primitive man (aka Da).

Many more family trips and childhood adventures will follow, but having given a glimpse of what Ma and Da were like, I think it's about time I mentioned how the woman from the North met and married the man from the South.

# Chapter 5
# Ma and Da Meet and Marry

As you can imagine in post-Second World War rural Ireland (that's about ninety-eight per cent of the country), the social scene was not a lot to write home about. Family get-togethers involved supplies of home-grown and home-cooked or home-baked food (of course), bottles of Smithwicks, Guinness or Harp for those with a taste for yeast and barley in various disguises or Poteen if potato was your fancy, and, of course, gallons of tea for those wanting to refrain from the temptations of Lucifer and be guided by the gospel according to priest or minister. Depending on location and family talent, home-grown music of various degrees of standard and listenability would outplay chatter, moaning, crying and rip-roaring laughter. As the most dependable form of transport was on foot, it wasn't surprising that get-togethers involved the same old faces week in, week out.

Then there was the local dinner dance — a pseudonym for a band playing Irish country waltzes accompanied by sausage and chips in a basket. This may be seen as a basic night's entertainment in millennium Ireland and Britain in local working men's clubs, traditional sports clubs and clubs with a political party name paint-scrolled above its door, but for the likes of Ma and Da this was about as exciting as it got on the social front. This was the meeting place of boy and girl, man and woman. Gayness hadn't been 'invented' in rural Ireland, so though flirtatious eye contact would have taken place amongst the existing gay community, fear of identity and ostracising (at the very least) put self-preservation at the top of any gay's list. Religious-indoctrinated suppression of the gay psyche, therefore, led to one distinct group of heterosexuals at a dinner dance — girls and women dancing with each other on one side of the social club hall whilst boys and men gawked, sneered and lusted after them on the other.

As Da had moved to Derry in the North from Letterkenny in the South (compass bearings have no bearing here) to serve his apprenticeship in turning and milling on the Derry shipyards, he was then a mere sixteen miles away from the woman he would meet, marry and spend his remaining days with. Such a distance was not easy to cover in fifties Ireland — especially on public transport, yet it made the 'meeting' all the more fate-driven.

As it happened, the first time Bertie's eyes met Minnie's was at a barn dance held by Aghnaloo's Young Farmers Society (which incorporated the area of Drumalief). What Da was doing travelling to such a distance to such a venue from the dizzy heights of The Maiden City of Derry with a few pals is not clear. What *is* clear is that he exchanged a few words with her in his Donegal brogue at the end of the night and was instantly attracted. Ma was more taken by the mysteriousness of a stranger from 'foreign' shores who had already gained a degree of independence by moving to Derry. Just like in the black and white movies of Hollywood, Da was the man who was the stranger, the traveller, 'experienced', whilst Ma was the home bird, the untravelled, the innocent. The strange mating and courting rituals at the time didn't so much as have a sniff of the online, speed-dating game played out today, so Da left without any real hope of seeing this redhead again. Ma was too practical to think of any possible reunion, so continued to look out for the man of her dreams from the limited resources of the northern hills of County Derry and the western slopes of County Antrim.

Fate twisted her mythical wand again though, six months later — this time at the Downhill Hotel, only half a dozen miles from the primary encounter. Just as the first event was instigated by the all-powering concerns of the Church, the celebration of harvest thanksgiving, so was the second, the celebrating of the crucifying and resurrection of Christ at Easter. The non-believers in the congregation of both, and of similar calendar landmarks, clearly appreciated the spirituality of believers as they could reap the benefits of the associated social life. I did too, with Brownie and Cub Scout camping weekends and Christmas bazaars as a child, Bible class outings to the seaside resort of Portrush as a teenager and the regular barn and dinner dances as an adult. The Church was quite content with its congregational mix as its bank account swelled as a result of such events — a pound was a pound regardless of whose pocket it emerged from. It is fair to say that Ma and Da were both believers — if only for accepting there was a heaven and hell; and that an almighty looked over their actions and deemed them sinful or otherwise and for saying the Lord's Prayer on a regular basis (or at least for forcing us wee ones to say it on a daily basis).

Da later confessed that he had hoped to see Ma for the second time at the Downhill Hotel's Easter Saturday dinner dance. He knew this was Ma's neck of the woods and had guessed that the local female talent would be there to show off their post-war dresses and hairdos. Ma, on the other hand, had all but forgotten about the brief moment of eye contact five months earlier with this outsider and had her eye on Jimmy Watson who she saw virtually every day as he waved and smiled from his muck-splattered Massey Ferguson with the silver-coloured, milk-filled missiles on the trailer behind. Although the prospect of being a farmer's wife was not Ma's idea of marriage, the familiarity of place and face encouraged her to look no further than the end of her nose. She had also witnessed close school friends meet someone from outside the boundaries of Limavady to the south and Coleraine to the north, and didn't fancy experiencing the sense of alienation of living well beyond what was recognisable and common as they had. How typical of Fate to use her close cousin Irony, to act on her behalf and toss her prey into an environment that was totally unfamiliar and foreign six months later, despite the instinctive fears to avoid such change.

So Ma sat with her own folk in the hotel's dance hall hoping for Jimmy Watson to arrive and ask her to dance. The hope, though, was unfounded as it was well known that Jimmy kept himself to himself and rarely attended such functions after his father had died the year before last. He clearly felt the whole impact of his new role as the head of the household, so would constantly find some job or other to do for his ma in the house, to do in the outhouses that circled the yard or to do for the livestock in the hedge-marked fields beyond. However, as the accordion, banjo and drums kept the partygoers' foot-tapping, and their heads nodding rhythmically to the sounds of Irish country sounds of Philomena Begley, Big Tom and the Mainliners and Brendan McIvor, Ma soon dealt with any feelings of disappointment (as she has always had done) and moved on and allowed some of the other local menfolk to swing her around the polished floor to one waltz and quickstep after another. She just enjoyed things for the moment; an attitude that we can easily lose sight of today with the clever techniques of advertising forever whetting our appetite with products and a lifestyle to make our future more comfortable, more hi-tech and somehow better —

and in turn making it increasingly difficult to take pleasure in what we have in the here and now!

Unknown to her though, was that Da had arrived and had been watching her for quite some time from the shadows of the corner next to the fire exit. He was prepared, she was not. So when he nervously ventured towards her after being continuously badgered by his trio of amigos from the 'big city' of Derry, he still held the ace card of surprise over Ma. The shock on her face quickly subsided to delight. Words were few and far between during their years together and this night was no different. The natural connection on the dance floor was evident for those who paid them any interest — this was just the beginning. It is also worth noting that their synchronicity on the dance floor led to them winning a number of dance competitions years later!

Courtship was short and swift — five months to be precise. Clearly, their synchronicity was not limited to their feet. The simplicity of their wedding in Limavady Presbyterian Church mirrored their humble backgrounds with only family and close friends attending the service. A basic, but nevertheless homely, spread of meats, salads, sandwiches and home-baked bread, washed down with well-brewed tea was what greeted the guests back in the red-brick house in Drumalief.

It was only when the welcomed stronger beverages of beer, gin, vodka and whiskey were let loose out of their bottles did the real celebrations begin.

Unfortunately for the newlyweds, a honeymoon of two nights in Mrs O'Gara's Bed and Breakfast overlooking the sands of Ballybofey in County Donegal beckoned — so they weren't to witness Auntie Silvia's giggle-ridden rendition of Jim Reeves' 'I Love You So', Uncle Billy's card tricks show, Aunt Jean and Uncle Sammy's quickstep waltz or the raucous laughs that roared into the wee hours of the next day.

The honeymoon of two days was filled with walks along windswept miles of long beaches and up and down heather-blossomed hills — intermitted by home-cooked meals at Mrs O'Gara's and consummation of marriage wherever it could be had. Sex before marriage was not an option for this typically moralistic couple. For many couples at this time, the liberation of physical intimacy that marriage vows gave was immeasurable. It seems that the power that this cultural belief or attitude towards sex (one of many) can be so enormous to those who are influenced by it — even if there is no real conviction to the foundation of faith behind it. This power can then allow the newly married couple to feel legitimately released to perform freely and frequently the same act that was so frowned upon before the religious ceremony. Even if this attitude doesn't make sense to some in today's more secular society, the adhering to what was seen as 'right' in Ma and Da's time is admired in many circles.

The joys of the wedding and bliss of the honeymoon were soon shoved away by reality's

81

stubborn stone. Why is there so often such a gulf between the good times and the continuous grind of work and home life? Is this the gods' way of getting us to appreciate such quality episodes in our lives? To ensure we keep our feet on the ground and don't get above our station? To confirm to us that we civilised beings need structure, routine and patterns in our lives? Whatever reason we afford ourselves to believe, we don't usually like the sense of 'fall' that reality forces us to experience after a sense of 'high'. What it usually means for us is that we take time to adjust to our return to actuality — and the more difficult the 'fall', the more time needed for adjustment.

As a child, the horrible 'fall' when having to leave the Banana slide at St Columb's park after the exhilaration of trying to out-slide me brother and sisters, or the 'fall' after the sweet-tasting can of Coke had dried up, or the 'fall' after the rain had blown its whistle to end the fantastic two-hour football game played over the Tins, was depressing, but it never seemed to last very long. The irony lay in that the lack of reasoning powers I had as a young child had a favourable outcome as it didn't allow me to dwell on the disappointment that reality brought or to respond in a lengthy uncontrollable fit of frustration that confusion can bring. Instead, it allowed me to deal with it in some unconscious way so that I was able move on to something else (Ma's approach rubbed off). It never took long to forget about the slide, the Coke or the game then. It's only now as an adult that the 'fall' can linger on and on if I let it — old Mr Rationale can let this happen. Instead of being able to deal with the fact that the great Guinness-fuelled karaoke party is over by telling meself that there will be another one to look forward to, me brain will hark after the 'moment' that has come to an end and resist the reality of the next day at the workplace. Child innocence has certainly got its strong points.

Now Ma and Da were officially Mr and Mrs Kennedy, they would have loved to have started married life in their own abode and to create a home for their future family — they had no plans for how many children they would like to have. However, a lack of money and an ill mother (Da's) meant they made the relatively short car journey from Ballybofey to Letterkenny and moved into the tiny house at 57 Main Street with Da's parents. Early married life was certainly not what either had expected. Ma was now looking after a frail and ill old woman she barely knew and living in an environment she was alien to without transport to visit family or friends — but adopting her usual 'just get on and do it' attitude meant that she didn't dwell on the negatives. Having to wait on a cranky and impatient mother-in-law only added to her general challenge. So, getting on with daily chores gave her the positive mindset that always held her in good stead. Waiting for her beloved Bertie to arrive on a Friday evening from his working week in Derry helped to lift any clouds of gloom, though privacy was always hard to come by in the tiny two-bedroomed cottage. Downstairs had purely a small room to cook in and a slightly larger room to sit and eat in. No television and no radio meant that there were only two types of sounds — those of chores such as cleaning or cooking, and those of voices. At least frequent visitors to the cottage who came to check on Da's ma during the day and early evening meant that Ma wasn't drowned by the silence — Da's da wasn't much of a talker. As they had married in July, Ma also had the comfort of long hours of daylight — at least for the first month or so.

Da lived in digs in Derry during the week as it was cheaper than travelling back and fore. Staying in Derry also gave him the opportunity to take on any overtime that was to be had. His desire to earn and save enough as soon as possible kept him going during this unromantic start to marriage. He was a good self-motivator and a very hard worker — I suppose work was a good distraction from the worry of his ma's poor health and likely death. He certainly wanted to make the most of the weekends at Letterkenny so created as many opportunities to take his new wife out and about in the surrounding landscape. Although Ma was used to the views of farmland and distant mountain ranges in Drumalief, the glorious mountains of Donegal and the sloping hills surrounding the bending currents of Lough Swilly gave her a sense of the fresh romanticism she had imagined married life would be.

The 'old woman' quietly passed away in the dark

hours of a damp Thursday November evening and was buried in the Church of Ireland graveyard in Letterkenny on the following Sunday. There was no money to pay for a tombstone — hence the 'find the grave' trip years later. By this time Da's da was becoming weaker of old age so it was agreed that Ma and Da would remain with him until they had enough money put aside for a house of their own. They had always planned to buy a house in Derry as this was where Da worked and it was also a more convenient distance from Ma's own folk in Drumalief and Limavady. In the March of the following year, they purchased 43 Alfred Street, in the Four Streets, in the Waterside area of Derry — accompanied by Da's da and a baby on the way.

The tiny, terraced house at number 43 was at the bottom of the street which gave the luxury of planning permission for a garage to be built a few years later. Despite the three bedrooms being relatively spacious when they first moved in (well, two of them were), and being a sheer comfort to what the cottage in Letterkenny offered, it became clogged, cramped and conflict-ridden by the time eight children arrived seventeen years later. Da's da only lived for three months after the Derry move so the building of the Bertie and Minnie dynasty truly began when the firstborn arrived in the November — the first of five births within the four walls of Number 43.

# Chapter 6
## Mina, the Firstborn

So at the top of the pile was Mina the first girl, and named in a sense after our ma, Minnie. It was certainly common practice in the Four Streets to name the first child after their ma or da. Opposite the front of our house were Big Jim and Wee Jim, and Big John and Wee John, whilst at the rear were Big Cahal and Wee Cahal. I think it just made it longer to say their names, and anyway, if any of us were referring to our mates it would only be Jim, John and Cahal as I was unlikely to be talking about any da of theirs. I don't know why, but if me own da was around, he would always ask if it was Big or Wee I was talking about. What happened to context and simply working out who was the protagonist? I think Da was just trying to indoctrinate us in his own subtle way — it would only annoy our happiness (typical Derry expression) to respond to his whim for detail and so it became easier to use the Big and the Wee. There was something both incestuous and potentially confusing about this sort of naming in Ma's eyes that she couldn't accept or get her head round, so she reached a compromise with tradition and came up with Mina.

Mina was a pure redhead like a number of our cousins — it was obvious that there was a strong Scot influence on Ma's side of the family — four of six of her own family in Drumalief were identified by the typical Scot copper noddle. She was quite a quiet girl who had Ma's homely aspirations and as she was the firstborn, she had plenty of practice in mothering when helping Ma out for years with her younger siblings. I know that she would often feed me, bath me and change me, but I had very few dealings with her after I had reached the age of remembering that, so that contact was hidden away in me subconscious somewhere. I didn't feel I really knew her and therefore struggled to feel a connection. The fact that she left the Irish shores (like so many others in Ireland) to find work in London by the time I was eight, only served to create a chasm in our sibling bond.

Vague snapshots and stories of Mina's presence in me psyche are summed up by four headlines: Coal Bunker, Secretarial Course, Soldier and London — in that order. When Mina was about two-and-a-half years old she would often go missing and increase Ma's anxiety levels. There weren't that many places to hide in a small, three-bed terraced house but Mina managed an ace one — the coal bunker.

Leading from the tiny scullery was the great outside — a narrow concrete backyard that was only four foot wide for the first six foot then opened to eight foot wide for a couple of more feet, before the vast expanse of eleven foot. The house scullery and bathroom exterior walls ran for the first eight foot on the yard's left — painted in a magnificent Cornish cream with the remaining eight foot being flanked by the emerald-green-painted shed. The right side was towered by the ten-foot-high garage wall, though at Mina's eye level, the four-foot-long wooden coal bunker and the two-foot-long metal coal slack box would have met her gaze. The far wall with its rarely opened or unlocked blue door was in keeping with the garage wall in terms of its height but it had its uniqueness in the jagged bits of glass that had been cemented into its tapered top. This so-called burglar-proof security system was not one of its kind in the neighbourhood — every backyard wall had at least one of them. I'm sure the local cat population just laughed at this system as they calmly prowled from yard to yard to leave their runny messes. In many ways the backyard had a claustrophobic and cold feel with its high Mayan ball-court-high perimeter walls and the lack of the sun-god rays fingering its flooring. However, it was freedom from a house filled with siblings and parents and it was the stadia for many a sporting fixture for me and Paul. They weren't quite of Mayan ceremonial proportions, but hard fought nevertheless.

The coal bunker residing in the backyard was the same for all households in the Four Streets and apart from the bathroom, scullery and kitchen, was probably the most used space in the home. It was either Ma or Da who, generated by fear and obsession (of the fire going out) would haul heaped shovelfuls of uneven chunks of coal or more evenly sized pieces of slack from its own bunker to the homely coal fire in the kitchen. The thought of the fire dying out was just unthinkable. Da had many a mini heart attack when discovering that the fire was on its last legs — though this was only when he hadn't been around to monitor the pace of the fuel burning and estimating the length of life left in it before petering out. Of course, he was concerned that the back boiler positioned behind the fire wouldn't be heated and therefore there wouldn't be hot water in the house. None of us kids ever made the sequential connections between bunker, coal, fire, boiler, tap and hot water, so I guess this was another one of those taken-for-granted parent things that you would only think about when you're an adult and responsible for your own hot water and that for your own offspring. Yet another delayed and silent appreciation for what Da did.

It was deemed unsafe to keep a bucket of coal or slack on the hearth in the kitchen (there was forever a young pair of inquisitive hands in the hunt for new species of mischief), so every time fuel was needed there was a trip outside. The draught that inevitably attempted to obtain squatter's rights, by way of a quick blast, was bearable in the not-too-hot Irish summer months but pure bitter frost-bite-cold for the other nine months. You didn't have to hear that Ma or Da had ventured out to the bunker, you just felt the consequences of the trek. There was no door between the kitchen and step down to the scullery, just a rectangular opening — so I guess the draught couldn't resist the invitation it received.

As for Mina, the step down to the scullery and a further step down to the backyard was the equivalent of a play park to the likes of her, so it was no surprise that she made the exploration to the great outdoors and to the unlocked coal bunker. Despite Da's obsessive-compulsive disorder with security, he deemed the high perimeter walls as protection enough against coal theft and didn't put a padlock on the coal bunker. The fact that it was frequently visited anyway meant that it would have been a greater hassle to continually play around with locks when stocking the hungry kitchen fire with sustenance.

The constant hoarse-whispering voice of the bunker constantly tempted Mina to its unlocked jaws and undaunted darkness inside, filled with heaps of black gold. It wasn't just getting inside that was the objective of the expedition, though this might have been the case on the first trip, but it was the taste of the coal. Poor Ma on that first occasion.

She let Mina wander out of the scullery door and play in the backyard as she often did — it was completely hemmed in by high walls. All Ma had to do was peep out of the door now and then to check on her, and on any trespassing cat. After a short while though, she looked and couldn't see her. Normally, when she couldn't see her at a glance, she would then have to go up the yard a wee bit to see if she was around the corner of the bathroom wall as the front of the shed was set a few feet back from this corner — and merely pick her up and bring her within eyeshot. This day she gave out a panic cry as Mina wasn't there. She checked the whole yard but didn't find her. She then ventured inside, thinking that she must have come back in without noticing her — but she wasn't in the scullery, bathroom or kitchen which were the only rooms she could have had access to. Without getting too panicky (Ma's sense of reasoning was always her regulator of emotions) she retraced her steps with greater application than previously — this time with a result. As she stepped out over the scullery threshold and into the backyard, her eyes were lower than previously as she wasn't looking up the yard. She noticed the coal bunker door ever-so-slightly ajar. She opened it wide and was utterly shocked to see Mina sitting comfortably in amongst the shiny black coal, her brightly coloured knee-length dress and white ankle socks covered with blotches and smears of black coal. To add to the occasion, she was doing her best to eat a chunk of the stuff. Her hands and face were clearly the colour of a Welsh miner after a twelve-hour shift down Blaenavon pit, yet her sense of contentment was undoubtedly not a fair reflection of such a miner.

Ma realised that someone (either her or Da, as no one else ventured in there) had left the latch off and

Mina had done a bit of her own exploring on a rare sunny, Derry summer's day. Despite the obvious lesson to be learned by this mishap of securing the coal shed, Ma found Mina on a number of other occasions in it — again very happy with her secret dark place amongst mountains of her favourite black delicacy! Whatever reprimanding went on, it didn't act as a deterrent. Da was eventually ordered to fix a padlock and that was the end of that feasting.

Mina's secondary school remains a blank to me but after she had left Clondermot Secondary modern I remember bits about her secretarial course at Derry Technical College and her first job working as a clerical assistant for an accountancy firm — well, I mean, secretary. She practised all the skills she had learned at school — typing, accounts and shorthand, but it was shorthand that drew me attention. I didn't see her at work so I didn't see any typing or accounting, but I was mesmerised by the squiggly writing on a number of notepads which lay around the house from time to time. The fascination that these nonsensical lines could actually mean something was not so much about the fact that they represented a foreign language (even extended vowel sounds used in mainland Britain was a foreign language to us in Ireland) but more that they represented a secret code. I would dreamily be taken to this Morse code by a frantic US marshal desperate for reinforcements to see off bare-chested Sioux warriors or a code used by James Bond to transfer vital information about Russian intelligence. I would often try and copy the squiggles and gain some understanding of them, but there were so many of them and so many that looked the same, that it was nigh on impossible to get to grips with them. Mina had no desire to waste her time on teaching one of her wee brothers so I flew the white flag in surrender — but I was so keen to be like the men of action in films that I ended up creating me own shorthand with messages for General Custard and MI5; 'surrounded by five hundred strong Sioux', 'reinforcements needed', 'Captain Lebrov in London tomorrow', 'meeting No.1 at 16.00'. No one else would have been able to decipher the coded language, but then that made it all the more special. Mina's typical retort of "ahemmmmm" when she took a peek at me handiwork on one of her pads was annoying — but most feedback from any of me big sisters was filled with criticism and negativity. I didn't look for praise but getting it would have been great. I was not surprised to find that receiving praise in later life would be overwhelming, though very satisfying. I'd like to think I'm tackling this element of me 'conditions of worth' as Carl Rogers would put it and therefore much more accepting of positive responses from those who give it.

Not long after I became aware of Mina earning money doing office work, came the headline news that she was bringing a boyfriend for Sunday tea. The ripple effect was unbelievable. Of course, I didn't know that this boyfriend was coming to our house till after the usual Sunday dinner feast and even after the passionate Brian Moore had talked us boys through the glorious Big Match. Arsenal had beaten Southampton 2-1, courtesy of the winner by Scot Frank McClintock from a corner. I was on me usual fever pitch high after watching the Gunners win, so when Ma announced that Mina was bringing a fella home for tea and that he was a British soldier, me adrenal gland continued to work overtime to contain the imbalance of excitement.

Before the deployment of the British Army to the streets of me homeland, me head had been filled by the heroes on the black and white screen in the corner of the kitchen. The dull and robotic Germans, the scheming and torturing Viet Cong and the ruthless and cold Japanese had all been ruthlessly despatched by the three Richard 'Lionhearts' — Richard Harris, Richard Burton and Richard Widmark. Their metal, muscle and mental astuteness were qualities I could only dream of and wish for. I would imitate their macho qualities in and out of doorways and parked cars on the Four Streets, up and down the dark and filthy lanes and on the infamous battlegrounds over the Tins. There was no uniform or replica gun to show any random onlooker that I was captain, sergeant or lieutenant, or that I was in combat and in the middle of major skirmishes to win back pilfered territory. Me superb weaving in and out of 'bombed' buildings, me clever rolls into 'tank-produced' earth craters and me deadly accurate shooting from me double-hand-held 'wooden' machine gun would let the occupied natives (said onlookers) know that I was one of their lethal allies fighting to bring about their emancipation.

The actual telly, with its 'expansive' choice of three channels (BskyB hadn't begun its global domination), made warfare look tough and dangerous yet trouble-free and do-able — making the soldiers distant and austere yet down to earth and approachable. Their carefully laid plans were clever and complex yet unpretentious and uncomplicated. The fantastical images in me young head that were conveyed via the magic screen were still illusionary snapshots when I was in me own pretend conflict. It was only when the British Army were deployed during the Troubles and I saw the jeeps, Land Rovers, lorries, Saracens and foot soldiers parade pass the top of me street, on their way to being housed in the naval quarters of Ebrington barracks only a stone's throw away, did war seem different. It became very scary and real.

I still felt excited by the British Army's landing, yet the tension polluting the Derry air by hundreds of grown-ups who had braved the dreary drizzle on that particular day denoted that here was a kind of war that I wouldn't be able to switch off from; it wasn't like a war on the telly. This would be a war that I was strangely part of but didn't fully grasp the meaning of. It was years later before I *did* grasp the significance of this day and of the huge political and cultural changes that their landing triggered.

The faces of the soldiers were young (though old to me at the time), grave and motionless — more like the German soldiers who guarded the POW camp of Colditz than the jovial, smoking and friendly British prisoners of war who faced adversity with spirit and passion. I couldn't quite figure out if these British soldiers were the enemy or the ally. I did what all we kids did, and didn't ask questions, but as the adult silence was suffocated by the noise of parading armoured vehicles, I was left floundering in the unknown. I did (again) what I always did (and still do) to overcome such struggles and gave focus to something that I deemed familiar — so I carefully scanned the soldiers' uniform.

I was always fascinated by the uniforms of me heroes — the ones who were in combat gear and carried out the dangerous missions and adventures and not the smart badge-splattered uniforms of the officers who sat around tables or danced around a ballroom with a pretty woman to a polka or waltz. Fighting and killing were much more a preference to the passive and 'feminine' attributes of talking and dancing. I was chuffed to only see the 'hero' types marching past me and peering out of jeeps and lorries. How did the officers get to the barracks? It must have been by helicopter. The khaki tunics and trousers were made of tough material to withstand all combat terrain and climate and mirrored the tough frame beneath; the shin-high black boots were crisp and shiny clean as they rhythmically thumped on the tarmac road — hundreds at the same time; the hard-as-nails green helmets worn on the head only served to heighten the clone effect and remove almost all signs of individuality — variations in height were the only real peculiarity. It was the actual guns that I spent most time peering at — big, black and heavy with bullets so that they had to be held by both hands across the body. The procession wasn't as long as the Orange Order parades, I'd witnessed many times before whilst standing at the top of Alfred Street, but it went on for some time — long enough for the silence of mouths, roar of engines and thudding of boots to make me turn cold and gradually hide behind the legs of Da. I would also hide like this when the Donegal pipers with their great black busbies that hid any sign of friendly face beneath them, marched past on one of the Twelfths. They would be gone in a matter of seconds, whereas the soldier march was never-ending. I wanted to flee back down the street well before they had passed but I was frozen to the spot — mainly from the unreal sight before me but also from the eerie emptiness that lay further down the empty street behind me; all houses had evacuated its human contents so that the latter could wonder at the war spectacle at the top of the street. There was no way I was going to head down the street with no one else about apart from whatever evil spirits that me mind would automatically conjure up. When it was over, I returned with Ma, Da and the rest of the family to the house — I looked at me friends and their faces said the same as mine — 'I'm not coming out for a bit' we needed to feel safe in our houses once more.

It was obvious that there was serious, adult stuff in the air. Me and Paul never stuck around for long when we sensed this — instincts seem to always tell us young ones that a situation was not to include our participation in, or contribution towards. Well, we would probably be more like an annoying distraction I suppose. I guess it was our way of subconsciously remaining as innocent as possible and to put the brakes on growing up too fast. Of course children's access to happenings in the global world of today has removed all brakes from growing up. So growing up happens much more quickly, whilst brutally removing a child's safety in innocence well before I lost mine. So me and Paul sleeked off to the front sitting room to play some board game, marble game or to make up a game.

Even though the kitchen was just on the other side of the front sitting room's wall, it was impossible to hear anything being said, talked about or shouted by the adults on the other side. The fact that doors were always kept shut for "don't let the heat out!" reason, meant that whatever room you were in had its own secluded ambience, without intrusion from whatever was going on in other rooms. In contrast, me house today, and for many years, rarely has any of its room doors shut and I think this gives a greater fluency of autonomy than the restricted space of me childhood — sanctuary can still be obtained by simply closing a door when desired. Nevertheless, when I visited me ma in later years, I'd be taken back to this secluded feeling as she still liked every door in the (new) house to be closed.

The sitting room itself had its own mystical qualities, with its monastery-like silence, its minimalistic formal furnishings and prayer-like sense of spirituality to allow us to escape the adult world in the room next door and also the fractured world in the street outside the narrow window. The room had a red tweed settee that faced a typical grey-tiled fireplace and hearth. Two matching armchairs sat at attention on either side of the hearth and guarded the three-bar electric fire that blocked the view of its adversary — the grate of the coal fire. Da's frugal attitude meant that three bars were never switched on and only in extreme circumstances were two bars allowed to come alive. Trying to have a sneaky bar on was *real* risky as he would frequently pop his monitoring head in to check. Quickly switching a bar off when we could hear him approaching was futile as a bar would take absolutely ages to change from burning red to cloud grey so evidence of the 'sin' was always blatantly obvious. The usual chastisement would be about cost and unnecessary heat, and would always contain his favourite and only swear word 'bloody'.

Me and Paul obviously needed a safe place to be in after the army procession. The fact that Ma and Da and the older family members weren't any good at hiding their own fears emphasised that the future of Derry and beyond was an uncertain and unstable one, double reason to be in a safe place. The sitting room was also a place where child-contemplation took place. Unlike the Irish monks over the centuries where education, faith and godliness were contemplated in peaceful settings — imaginative play was our concern. Something inside us dictated that we weren't to mirror the combative nature of the scenes we had just witnessed on the streets earlier, so soldiers or plastic Indians were not thought about or talked about. In their place our minds searched for something more passive to occupy our refuge, so Ludo was chosen. We still needed something with a competitive edge or play would have been a waste of time to us. We also revelled in the objective of taking captive your opponent's pieces (men) for as long as possible as part of the overall aim of the game — though the irony of war simulation was lost on us. It was almost tragic that the sitting room wasn't to remain a needed safe place, even though the Troubles in Derry escalated over the following six years (before we moved from Alfred Street). This was because we and everyone else in Derry got so used to the scenes of war and therefore the psychological need for a safe place was, ironically, no longer warranted. I guess the same attitude happens in most war zones all over the globe — people adapt to what's happening and 'get on' with their lives as best they can. It's only when watching 'snapshot' images of war on our television screens from a position of relative calm that we can't understand how people can 'live' in these places.

So, Ma's announcement that Mina's soldier boyfriend was coming at five o'clock meant that I had one and half hours to think about him and to think about what having a boyfriend meant. I knew that it would be interesting to see what Ma's movements would be like with this visitor in the house.

I had seen some squaddies in their civvies walking about Ebrington Terrace, in the vicinity of the Four Streets, inside and outside Casonie's chippy and flitting between the Bookies and Ebrington Bar which were a matter of yards apart. All of these locations were within a 'safe' zone from Ebrington Barracks which housed them. Of course, I'd never seen one squaddie on his own. They were always in large groups — not just because they would have off-duty at the same time but being isolated in Derry, even in so-called safe zones, was too risky. It would only take a squaddie to be in the wrong place at the wrong time to having his head kicked in by a gang of bored proddies (Protestants) or hate-filled Fenians (Catholics). A few black eyes, countless bruises and a sore head were preferable to a few bullets in the head — many gravestones are evidence of that.

In addition to the groups of squaddies, groups of young boys would keep to type and were always intimidating and menacing looking, just by their presence and size. I would usually avoid having to pass such a group — even if they were a proddy gang and I knew most of them. If I did pass near a gang, I'd avoid eye contact just in case someone took a dislike to being looked at and in their false sense of strength, lash out at me with a black Doctor Marten boot, or worse still, a steel toe-capped brogue shoe (they really hurt when they landed on a puny bone frame like mine). With the group of squaddies though, I always stared — fascinated by their short-back-and-sides hairstyles (longer than me own), their loudness and laughter, and more noticeable and intriguing, their funny accents. I'd only heard such voices on the telly — and that's where they 'lived', so having them on me own turf seemed odd, but fascinating, to say the least.

I imagined a cigarette hanging from the corner of Mina's fella's mouth or positioned behind his ear, ready for lighting and puffing at any given moment; and him looking smart, confident and speaking articulately. He'd also be nervous coming into our little house at the bottom of a hill, filled with people with foreign tongues in a land that was still alien and hostile to him — but trying his best not to show it. The macho soldier archetype doesn't allow for sentiment, weakness, embarrassment and shyness. The training, the superiors, the culture and macho peers batter this out of a young recruit in Catterick in order to instil the winning and 'we're the best' mentality — and ultimately to prepare them for combat wherever they'd be stationed. Stationed in Derry in 1970 where they were always walking targets for verbal abuse, broken bricks, petrol bombs or sniper fire meant that private, corporal, sergeant or commander had to show fearlessness, strength, invincibility and power once they donned the British Army uniform. Seeing them in civvies didn't change them — they were just the same. Would this fella be different away from his 'comfort zone'? Did he have family? Have brothers and sisters like me? Was he any good at football? What team did he support? Arsenal like me? Liverpool like Paul? Wolves like Robin? I never thought about him being *Mina's* boyfriend and what they were like together — I hated any romantic business in the films on telly. As far as I was concerned, such romanticism just seemed stupid to me young lad's head and spoilt the action, and weakened the hero. I couldn't bear seeing the hero captured, shot or beaten all because he had 'softened up' or got distracted — had allowed a girl to get to him! This narrow view would change in time.

Watching Ma, though, was clearly fascinating — she would have been a joy to any behavioural scientist's caseload or their research subject. When Granny or me aunts and uncles were due for tea there would be extra hoovering, dusting, cleaning and putting out of sight any drying washing (the clothes line of course was suspended from the kitchen's ceiling). This never made sense to me as Ma never let dust settle on any surface long enough to be seen and the lino floors were crumb-free and a perfection of shining slipperiness. No words of "it doesn't need doin'" from Da or me sisters would have the least bit of impact — in fact, they were likely to be greeted by a scowl that was full of irritation and resentment. When Ma set her mind to do something, that was it.

When Ma gave this response, we all knew that that was the end of any discussion — and dare help someone who dared push her further. Her face would be a mass of pointedness — her nose was long and pointed anyway, but somehow the rest of her face would take on this witch-like force, whilst her eyes would extend well beyond her eyelids. After a succession of fiery verbals that defended her duties, she would slate all of us for questioning her (the individual who kicked-started this never got the deserved focus of the back lashing) and then highlight the fact that she hadn't asked us to do anything! This was finished off by a mighty frown and stone-like face that stared for what seemed ages. No one would speak — and she would then finish off with "There, I'm just tellin' you how it is". This statement was clearly a powerful one — one that didn't require any response, one that allowed her to vent her irritation at being challenged, one that drew a line under the whole matter so confrontation was ended, and yet one that was so sophisticated that it came across that she wasn't really judging us or having a go at us — even if it felt like it. I would know that everyone else, would be feeling the same as me — awful and guilty — even if we didn't know why. It was probably something about knowing Ma having enough to do each day to make our lives as comfortable as possible without complaining, so anything that upset her felt bad.

So at half past four the doorbell rang, followed by a blanket of frozen air that rooted everyone to the position they were in. Me and Paul were in the middle of a game of blow football, with cheeks puffing away before being quickly sucked in to reload the blowing power. The plastic brown ball suddenly stayed where it was as the blowing and sucking motions just stopped; the Family Circle biscuit tin stopped in mid-flight as Ma's grip tightened on its rim as she reached it down from its child-safe perch; Da's licked, wet thumb stood motionless unable to turn the next page of last night's previously read *Belfast Telegraph*; the giggling through the sitting room wall from Irene, Hazel and Val had died prematurely; even the telly seemed to want to join in with the silence as the 'Sunday Matinee' on ITV paused with the 'quiet' Milk Tray advert.

The whole house then listened as Mina rushed down the stairs before suddenly slowing her steps as she moved along the hallway and opened the vestibule glass door. There was another pause as she did the usual woman thing of adjusting her hair and swiping her hands down her cotton top and tweed skirt as if swatting away some imaginary dust; she was now ready to open the front door.

I wanted to see what he was like so I lifted the plastic ball in order to momentarily halt the match and so that Paul couldn't blow the ball into the back of my net and claim a goal while I was distracted. Paul was just about to shout something at me when in *he* came.

His tall slim frame adorned an unzipped brown leather jacket showing a light blue polo shirt, whilst his beige flared trousers more or less covered his brown brogues. He had short black hair and a thick but short moustache. I knew that his smart appearance wasn't just put on for Ma and Da's sake as I'd seen many others like him outside the barracks. I guess being trained to look smart whilst on duty was still part of the mindset when off duty.

Mina did the customary introductions to Ma and Da and I learned his name was Steve. By the time I heard his 'weird' accent (I'd no idea it harked from Hertfordshire, wherever that was) as he said, "I'm very pleased to meet you, Mr and Mrs Kennedy", me sisters had emerged at the kitchen's door frame with an excitement in their faces as if they were about to meet the likes of Rod Stewart. Mina then told Steve all our names. As if the clan that confronted him wasn't big enough of a shock for him, the front door opened and in came Robin. Saying that, I think having another bloke, albeit a few years younger than him, seemed to put him at ease a bit as he smiled back at Robin. Having little two-year-old Isobel toddling about also seemed to give Steve something else to distract him from the usual uncomfortable feeling that goes with the territory of meeting your girlfriend's parents for the first time. He would be able to talk to Isobel in a more relaxed and playful way without any possible judgement or scrutiny taking place, whereas with Ma and Da he would be trying to impress them at every turn. He needn't worry about trying to reassure Da about the mythical father and daughter thing of being 'good enough' for his daughter as Da didn't have that bond with any of his daughters (or sons for that matter), but he wasn't to know that. It wasn't until tea was actually on the table about thirty minutes later that I got to see how he was with Da. Me and Paul were banished from the kitchen and sent packing into the sitting room shortly after his arrival because of one-too-many stifled giggles. We just couldn't keep our faces straight every time we heard his weird accent, so Mina ordered us out. It was pointless even trying to defend our case as we could see that Da was on the cusp of a blow-out anyway; his scowl had been developing ever since the first snigger. We quickly obeyed Mina and took our blow football game with us. The other three older sisters had entrenched themselves in Steve's company so at least we had the room to ourselves.

We didn't talk about Steve at all but moaned a bit about our 'unfair treatment' by Mina and her 'right' to chuck us out on the basis that her boyfriend was visiting. It was just another occasion that we felt hard done by, but getting back into another fiercely fought game of blow football soon allowed us to once again get over our angst. Paul managed to sneak that game 9-8. I'm sure me focus wasn't up to scratch owing to the 'visitor' behind the thick-bricked wall, but then again, it was probably the same for him. Most competitive games we played were evenly matched. It wasn't till later in our teens, and we had bought Subbuteo, that an imbalance became evident — he never landed a defeat on me!

We had agreed that when the shout came for tea being ready, that that would be the final whistle. So hearing Val's voice "come on, boys, tea's ready" as she stuck her head round the door brought an end to the one of thousands of Arsenal versus Liverpool grudge matches. In fact, the stadia for these grudge matches varied considerably for a whole host of games: blow football, long shooty over the Tins or on the beach, penalty shootout against Da's garage door, kerby using the road kerbs on the street, one-touch against the gable wall, and virtually every board game played on the floor, table or sofa. Anything that would allow points or goals to be scored gave us reason to compete.

Sauntering into the kitchen for tea, I could see that the drop-leaf table was fully extended to allow for the whole congregation to worship the gorgeous spread that Ma had created. It had seemed only a short time ago that the family had sat around the same table to devour the traditional three-course Sunday dinner. I was positioned on the far end with my back against the wall as usual but this time there was Robin in between me and Paul as Steve had been allocated his traditional spot that was next to Mina.

I wasn't interested in what the conversation was about but I was aware that the usual interrogation about heritage, family, life in England and such like had already been played out prior to tea. Typically though, Da always tried to bring the topic round to the Troubles and what Steve's experiences had been. Ironically, Da was the absolute expert on the Troubles in many ways anyway, as he listened to every news bulletin and watched every news item that frequented the airwaves and aerial waves. His persistence did pay off though, despite Ma's protestations and Steve's own avoidance strategies.

He relayed the account of when his foot patrol were on Craigavon Bridge, and came under fire from snipers positioned on the heights of Gobnascale. This sniper fire was a common event throughout the Troubles, and like many common events, it became uneventful and became embedded in our culture's norm. However, to hear about it at first hand and before it did settle into our cultural norm, made for interesting listening.

"Well, there were six of us; three one side of the bridge and three the other side. We were in staggered formation too as all foot patrols are trained to be in, heading west, or as you would call it 'over the Town'. I was in the middle carrying my rifle across my body and the box radio on my back; god, they're heavy buggers after you've carried them for a few miles. You're always a bit hyped up as soon as you step foot out of the barracks here next door, but even when you're out in the open like that you turn into an eagle. You watch everything and everyone but at the same time not to make it too obvious or intense. We're told to act relaxed and normal so that we don't scare everyone. Relaxed and normal are the last things we feel! You can't trust anyone. Everything looks suspicious the more you look at it. The basic training we did in Catterick, sure doesn't prepare you for walking the streets of Londonderry. You're like a moving target — and you know you could be shot at, at any second. Sorry, I'm probably boring you with all of this."

"Oh, goodness," Ma ushered, without any real decisiveness in her voice.

"No, no, you carry on son," was Da's interested retort.

No one else spoke — we were all too busy picturing the scene in our heads, but for the first time we were getting the sense of what was going on inside the man that wore the green uniform and who still felt an alien and a kind of trespasser in our town of Derry. So this particular 'alien' carried on.

"We were about halfway across when a rapid sound of gunfire like loud cracks in the sky rang out — I could hear a couple of rounds bounce off the iron. Shit! Oh, so sorry for swearing, Mrs Kennedy. Our corporal shouted for us to get down. Don't worry, there was no need for him to shout. I crouched down with my side against the side of the bridge. I'd heard of others talking about similar times when they'd been out on patrol but nothing prepares you for your first time under fire in an open space like that. I started to radio HQ immediately and report the gunfire and possible location and, before

I knew it, I could see that one of the choppers was heading out of the barracks and towards Gobnascale — they'd be there in sixty seconds. Our boys on the bridge couldn't fire back — there was nothing to see. That's the bloody snipers for you — they'd hide amongst the local civilians!

"My mate Chompy — he's called that because of the way he eats his food — was looking through his glasses but still couldn't see anything or anyone. The gunfire soon stopped as it always did, once the chopper got nearer, but the bridge was manic; people were screaming and running for cover and drivers drove as fast as they could. I've got to say, that that's been the scariest time I've had since I've been stationed here but I guess that's what I'm here for."

"I suppose there was a checkpoint set up on the bridge then eh?" Da asked. "There have been plenty of them about. I'm forever being held up there and even had to empty my boot once."

"Aye, I remember that," I spouted, and then felt my face redden as it always did when everyone's eyes were focused on my direction. I distracted meself from the spotlight by recalling in me own head, the checkpoint scenario that Da was on about.

We were heading off for the beach at Dunree in Donegal, just a short journey on the far side of Buncrana. Dunree was great for me and Paul. It was a typical beach in the Free State that was totally unspoilt. It had some huge sand dunes to roll down, lovely soft deep sand to dive all over the place in when playing 'long shooty', water that was crystal clear so any jellyfish could easily be spotted and avoided, rocks to explore for small fishes and crabs and a small army (Irish) fort that stood proud and at attention on the hilltop, keeping watch on everything and everyone that ventured on its territory below. Of course, there was the stretch of sheep-eaten grassland that divided the unofficial car park from the beach that was ample space for the traditional family picnic (though it was never called that — just 'tea') as well as just enough space for our own Wembley pitch in between the blobs of cow dung. It was inevitable that once Ma and Da decided (eventually after much boring adult debating) that it was Dunree that we were going to that day, that all these images of Dunree would flash across me mind. I knew that Paul would be thinking the same — we just wouldn't talk about it.

As per usual, it was about three o'clock before the Morris Oxford was packed with food, toys, us kids (me, Paul, Val, Hazel and baby Isobel) and Ma and Da. As per usual too, me initial adrenalin about going to the beach had subsided during the tortuous time between dinner and actually getting in the car, but would then resurrect itself once we were all crammed in it. I was in the back seat with me older sisters, Isobel on Ma's lap and Paul on the handbrake. Me and Paul had to take turns to sit on the long stick between Ma and Da. If we were on a steep hill and the traffic was moving slowly, then he'd have to balance himself on one of Ma's knees, whilst Isobel sat on the other. So when the car hit Duke Street (barely minutes into the journey) and Da announced that there was a checkpoint on Craigavon Bridge that tailed back to most of Duke Street, me heart just collapsed in despair and frustration — though it would have been worse if I'd been on the handbrake. Even though I would eventually be fascinated by the soldiers and their guns, at that moment in time I only felt a cavern at the pit of me tummy — glorious Dunree beach would have to wait a bit longer. There was even deeper despair at the possibility of the checkpoint holding traffic up so much that getting to Dunree at all was in jeopardy!

Da chose the queue that would take us on to the upper deck. This was one of those spontaneous decisions based on some primal instinct or feeling rather than some mathematical calculation of traffic speed — a decision that was pure chance, but one that you would have to live with and defend to the hilt despite any rational challenges from others if it didn't have a positive outcome.

It's amazing how our brains kick in to a competitive mode in these situations as everyone started to watch the line of traffic that took the 'other' route — the lower deck of the bridge in this case. Whilst all of us watched the traffic heading for the lower deck, I could see all of the 'opposition' were looking at us from inside their own cars and were watching us with fierce looks. It wasn't necessary to hear what they were saying because we were saying the same,

"Quick, Da, they're going faster than us."

"Aw no, we're going nowhere!"

"Great, now we're moving — just look at their angry faces!"

Eventually we were on the bridge and couldn't see the mob down on the lower deck. It didn't matter — at least for now anyway. I didn't know whether to look along the bridge, to the right of us, to the left of us or up at Gobnascale (with emphasis on the first and third syllables, so that there was rhythm in pronouncing it). There were British soldiers everywhere with their big guns and black camouflage paint on their faces even though it was broad daylight. I saw Charles Bronson use boot polish but it served the same purpose. I tried counting but gave up after fourteen as they kept moving about. I hadn't seen so many in action in one place, and so visible for everyone to see. I heard Da say to Ma that something serious must be going on; I could hear the usual delight in his voice to be caught up on something potentially dangerous. Ma just went her usual silent self. I was silent too.

Hearing huge booms in the air as bombs went off left, right and centre across the River Foyle as I played over the Tins was scary enough. They were much more deafening than any firework I got to hear in later years (fireworks were banned during the Troubles). But I was safe across the other side of the river when the bombs went off. Only once was I caught up in the thick of a bomb, but more on that later.

Being stuck on the bridge felt scary, and apart from Da's running commentary on actual events and on his usual fantastical possible events, our car was dead, without sound. Even the car engine seemed to empathise and couldn't be heard. In complete antithesis, the noise outside the car penetrated the silence inside it. The boys in camouflage were shouting orders to each other and shouting orders to the inhabitants of every car to stay in them. Saracens roared up and down the bridge like angry wildcats as they moved off and on the pavement, and constantly fought for stability. But the speedy loud chugging of two choppers, one at each end of the bridge, won first prize for the most deafening!

I could see the four lanes of traffic moving at a slug's pace. The sun had decided to add its extra heat to the situation, aided by its cousin clouds seemingly disappearing into thin air. There was now an un-Irish blue sky to be seen. This just made us kids even more uptight as our eagerness to get to the beach was filling our bodies with adrenalin — and this in turn filled our bladders. There is nothing worse than needing a pee and feeling the small ache that emerges, knowing that the ache is going to increase and increase. Knowing that Da would bite your face off if you were to mention needing a pee only made matters worse.

I tried to concentrate on the occupants of the other cars to take me mind off the bladder ache. I could see that Ford, Vauxhall, Chrysler, Austin and Mercedes cars were represented on the bridge and that a shade of blue was the dominant colour. Most cars either had a couple in them or were jam-packed with families — the contraception pill of the sixties hadn't swum across the Irish Sea to us yet. All car windows were opened wide to allow for as much air as possible so it was easy to see people's faces and read how others were coping with the delay to the beach. I knew everyone was beach bound as shops didn't open in Derry on Sundays, no religious service would be taking place in the middle of the afternoon and Derry folk always headed to the seashore when it was obvious that rain wasn't on the horizon.

I was feeling hot and could sense the thin layer of sweat on me skin and me blond hair beginning to dampen by the second. It's one thing being aware of me own hot body and hot head but it's distressing seeing it mirrored by everyone else around. It was even more distressing seeing other kids suffering more than me; a veil of resignation was evident. To top it all, some of me peers had made the fatal mistake of whinging too much or voicing that they needed a pee, and had obviously had a verbal bashing, or worse still, a slap from a parent or older sibling. The noise all around was still extremely loud so their bawls and cries appeared merely as a mime for any onlooker like me.

Even though it felt as though time and Da's car had stood still forever, it hadn't. I was having such a battle of focus between me bladder and the depression on others' faces, that I hadn't noticed we were now just two cars' away from the soldiers' checkpoint.

There was a whole swarm of them. Those who were not waving cars forward and checking driving licences were either crouched down on their haunches, standing almost at attention, or leaning on the bridge. All had a heavy rifle in their hand and were ready for action. In some ways it seemed a bit superfluous and futile as the IRA (it was always the IRA) had long gone after they'd done their business and were very unlikely to return once the men in green appeared in large numbers. They were just like an Apache raiding party who attacked a small US Army outpost on the outskirts of the main fort, who quickly slaughtered a few soldiers and then ran off back to the safety of the tribe. There was no way they were going to return once the army general sent out forty of his well-trained troops on horseback. What Indian braves or freedom fighters were going to come out and expose themselves to an enemy army that was far superior in numbers and weaponry? On top of that, the British soldiers' checkpoint strategy of checking driving licences was purely a waste of time — did they think that the freedom fighters were dumb enough to travel about at a time when they knew that a few sniper shots or a bomb blast would bring out the cavalry? So, all of us who wanted to get to the beach were then held up in queues of traffic so that an army corporal could check our das' licences, asked where we were heading ('an IRA training camp no less!') or at worst, be asked

117

to open the boot of their cars for a brief rummage, before being waved on. What was the point?

It was now our turn. Part of me wanted Da to be delayed a bit with questions and with having to open his boot because it would give me a pleasant feeling of goosebumps all over. Even though there was nothing to hide from the soldiers, there was always an element of fear running through me veins. What if they found something suspicious or something that Da shouldn't have had? Stupid questions, I know, but doubt does strange things to rational thinking. Another part of me wanted to finally get across the bridge, get through the area that was on the verge of the notorious Bogside, and out the Buncrana Road where Dunree beach beckoned. On this occasion, the corporal gave a glance at Da's licence to see that the photo matched the face looking at him, nodded and waved him on (Ireland has always been viewed by 'Mainlanders' as being decades behind the times, but it took Mainland Britain years after Ireland to have photos on their driving licences — ha).

Me sisters were almost swooning in the back seat at the bloke in the green uniform. I could never understand the female mentality of getting blushingly excited at a man in uniform; soldier, policeman, fireman or whatever. I know that it creates a bit of jealousy in me at the unconditional attention they get, and that they're obviously loving this attention. I never wore a uniform that boosted me ego or attracted girls' attention so I don't know what that's like. I do know that wearing the kilted uniform of Culmore Pipe Band as a drum major in me late teens made me feel special and onlookers would give me much attention, but this wasn't the attire to knock the girls off their feet or encourage a flashing of a leg (theirs not mine!) — never mind an eyelash!

By the time I'd daydreamed about the bridge scenario and how I got to relieve me bladder in a country lane, Da had stopped asking Mina's Steve questions and Ma's home-made fruit cake was looking at me with a wink of temptation. I had clearly switched off from the whole episode of Steve the soldier coming for tea — I had a good knack of zoning out when things got either awkward or boring. I had experienced both of these and before I knew it, Steve and Mina were out the door to spend some time together and the house got back to its normal Sunday evening — dead boring. I never saw Steve again and didn't know what happened to him or to him and Mina. The whole world of romance and adult relationships was something that I knew nothing about, and didn't want to know anything about. I'd seen too many battle-hardened heroes on the beloved black and white telly screen, being disarmed, trapped, softened, balded (Samson) and weakened by so-called romantic liaisons with the opposite sex to be in the least interested in 'adult stuff'.

Me own liaisons with girls of me own age (or thereabouts) seemed to be fun, had no hidden agendas or conspiracies — a culture far removed from that of adults. I remember me first kiss (aged five) with blond-haired Mary when at nursery — she had a lovely, sweet smile and a face dotted with light-coloured freckles. We spent about two days having a quick kiss every break time — we'd as quickly run away giggling from each other as we'd fleetingly 'met' in the first place. Then nothing happened on the third day. Synchronicity played out a perfect tune as we both just got on with interacting with others and with our own lives without any desire or need or attraction to kiss one another. There was no heartbreak, no victimisation, no emotional turmoil, no confidence-bashing — we simply 'moved on'. How easy was that to the end of a relationship? Of course I liked other girls in the early years of nursery school but they didn't result in any kissing escapades. In fact, it was about two years later before another girl crossed me lips — more of that later.

Well, I don't recall Mina ever having any other boyfriend over for tea — or that she ever had another boyfriend of any kind. What I do recall is how long she would spend in the bathroom and therefore how much aggro and tension and bad feeling she would create amongst the rest of the household. Despite what I would consider as living in a very modest terrace house compared to your average working-class home in the twenty-first century, I also knew that other folks didn't have what we had — an inside bathroom! The majority of houses had an outside toilet at the back of the backyard — why the farthest away from the house I ask? Any soul needing to relieve themselves in the winter had to dash through the rain or snow or wind or sleet or whatever dropped from the sky. God help anyone who was easily spooked by the thought of witches or ghosts or the bogeyman. The small beam of a torchlight would only serve to show you the way to the creepy hut of a toilet with its dodgy wooden frame and corrugated iron roof. It definitely wasn't enough to frighten any lurking figures from the 'other world' let alone any of this world's hungry rats that swarmed in from the nearby River Foyle and frequented the Four Streets at any time of day or night. I'm sure the rats just scoffed at any trembling one of us two-footed creatures who ran or tipped-toed or staggered their way to the supposed 'security' of the toilet shed. No one would know if a rat was actually in the toilet shed 'til they were already in it — too late!

So, if we ever complained about Mina's bathroom activities (I'm sure she could have been sponsored by Twyfords or Tiles 'r' Us), and we kids surely whinged, Da would put on his pulpit-looking face and preach that we should be grateful for what we had, compared to many others who not only had an outside loo, but didn't even have a bath other than a tin one. If Irene or Hazel or Val (not having access to the bathroom didn't evoke quite the same pain or anger for us boys) were brave enough or angry enough to tell Da that that was well and good, but that having a 'fancy' bathroom was no good if you couldn't get into it, Da would just do his usual poker-faced stare in resignation. Da never won a battle of words with anyone; not that he wasn't witty or clever with words, just that his wit or intellect lacked stamina or depth. I think his lack of compulsory education (typical of his youth in the educational environs of rural Letterkenny) was a sore point for him and made him feel quite inferior. I guess this sense of inferiority complex was (and still is in many quarters) a pretty common experience for those 'working class' parents who would strive to give their offspring the education they themselves didn't have — yet would then feel left behind and inadequate as their children would use a vernacular or a set of ideals or have a very different mindset to that of their own. Educational opportunities for their kids would often bring about qualifications and further development in the career ladder, of which they'd undoubtedly be proud of, but at a cost of feeling detached or subordinate or even embarrassed. Da, I think, felt all three of these. I would laugh at his pathetic posture and demeanour at such times — perhaps it was a bit of karma for his ogre-type ways? I didn't laugh in later life as I could recognise that for a man of such masculine qualities and tough exterior, being humiliated by the intellect of his daughters surely pierced his manhood.

What was even more infuriating for everyone about Mina's epic bathroom times was that she was absolutely emotionally and mentally removed from the high-voltage turbulence she triggered amongst her siblings.

She wouldn't retaliate but would simply walk past the raucousness around her — not with an air of royalty or pretentiousness, but with an expression of 'zoning out' to all around her. I never really saw her in any other mode of presentation other than remaining totally unfazed. Hazel's frustrations were probably the most intense and she would be the one who would blindly persevere in trying to get Mina to become 'aware' of her shortcomings and the consequential happenings of these — in the hope she would learn. Even Hazel's contorted and venomous red-haired face that would certainly scare the toilet-shed rats, and that would be inches away from Mina's expressionless countenance, did nothing to stir Mina into any movement or retaliation or even acknowledgement of what she was shouting at her about (for the millionth time!). Obviously, this just fuelled Hazel's fast-disappearing tolerance and her voice would then get louder and louder as Mina would begin to saunter away, totally unconcerned that the raging bull of Hazel was purple in the face. Da would then intervene with a shout that minimalised Hazel's — it would be his usual "Whad 'r' ye at?" This wasn't so much a question but a demand to shut up, and not because he had had enough of the shenanigans going on but because he didn't want to have the 'shame' of the neighbours hearing. This was something that Ma colluded with him about — the thought that others might think badly of our household, and in some perverse way, think that we were unchristian was mortifying for them. It's fair to say that this was not a mindset restricted to Ma and Da, but one throughout the Four Streets and throughout the streets of Derry in general.

We youth at the time just didn't get that false sense of decency and hypocritical respect, and would challenge that with much vigour and buccaneering attitude with utterances of "I don't care" or "so what, what the neighbours think", and so on. Then we same youth become adults and parents and adopted exactly similar attitudes — leaving our own offspring with the same rebelliousness as we had when in our youth. At what point do we kind of morph into our parents in attitudes such as this? Why do we lose that 'don't care' attitude when we know full well that we're turning into our parents in a way we used to despise? It's difficult in such times to counter Aristotle, Cicero or Locke's argument of determinism and that we don't have free will to choose our own attitude — this is how it is, this is how it's always been and this is how it's going to be!

It's fair to say too, that we always like to think we have made our own decisions, rules, attitudes and ways of being — it gives us empowerment and a sense of self-control. To think the contrary, leaves us where? Vulnerable? Anxious? Unstable? It's easy to see then how it's better to fool ourselves about self-determinism — especially when we're aware of so many other things around us that we have no control over — regardless of epoch we live in.

In terms of Mina and Hazel, it wasn't rocket science to work out which of the two had a greater sense of control of their lives when it came to the bathroom saga; Mina with her lack of self-awareness which verged on blissful oblivion or Hazel with her raging desire to instil some self-awareness in her, time and time and time again, but ultimately failing. There are some things that time just can't, or won't, change.

I guess being the eldest in the family brings its own responsibilities and pressure to be a kind of role model to us young 'uns. Apart from the bathroom tensions she created, she also took time out to help Ma with the endless list of daily chores as well as feeding us wains. As knitting was a typical pastime for girls her age, she also knitted many a garment for us too.

I don't recall having many dealings with Mina in my infant years — though I'm sure she can remember a fair few. What does stand out though was the announcement of her heading off to London, England. Well, I say announcement; it was more of the usual picking up scraps of conversations and the odd mention of London. Of course, Ma's exasperated demeanour and Da's extra-stern scowling face indicated something very serious was about to happen, and both of them weren't too happy about it. I can only fathom that most of the dead serious dialogue took place when I was in the depths of slumber. There's no way Ma would have allowed Da to break family etiquette and a sense of decorum by getting worked up about something like that in front of the likes of me and Paul. I reckon Ma could have been the new Bertram Thomas or Benjamin Franklin, such were her powers of diplomacy and mediation. Tensions can often run high amongst family members as there's often the 'blood inhibition effect' — meaning that a family member believes they can say what they like to a close blood relative as this notion of blood will prevent long-term relationship damage. It's almost an unconscious way of being that has its faith in unconditional blood connection regardless of hurt, blame or offence. So Ma's strategic manoeuvres were about keeping the damage of a family feud (and Da's temper, of course) to a minimum.

This 'family diplomatic policy' obviously worked as I never heard of or witnessed any family explosions — only the type set off by the IRA! In fact, it was partially because of the IRA's bombs and other sectarian comings and goings that brought about Mina's decision to seek pastures new in England. She certainly was the pioneer in our house in leaving all that she knew to venture across the Irish Sea — five of the rest of us, including me, followed in good time.

She was not leaving Derry alone though, as two of her good friends Kathleen and Bridget, were going with her. They'd all learned their secretarial trade in doing the likes of shorthand, typewriting and accounts at Derry Tech before working for either Thompson's solicitors or the council to boost their CVs. Kathleen had already had a sister who had set her roots in London and who endorsed the typical lyrics of London having 'streets paved with gold'. I overheard Ma reassuringly tell Da on one occasion that she'd have no problem getting a job — and she was right.

Me and Paul were typically not interested in big sister not being around or even had any notion of the huge decision this was for Mina and for Ma and Da. In fact, Mina's leaving was a very quiet affair as far as I was concerned. Da and Ma were going with her to Aldergrove airport — me and Paul watched them all get into the car from the dizzy heights of the sleepers that bordered the Tins whilst me other sisters waved frantically from the front door. We both watched as the Wolseley cruised over the hill of Alfred Street on its way to the airport (a place I could only imagine in my head). Once out of sight, we got on with a game of football. Something about the occasion entered our subconscious minds as we decided to be two London teams for the game — West Ham and Chelsea — we'd never done that before!

# Chapter 7
## Irene, the Second Born

If Mina refused to acknowledge her ways by ignoring the feedback she got from those around her, the next sibling in line, Irene, had a different approach — denial, and a more defensive rejection of any criticism. She also had a pretty rebellious nature to add to the explosive mix.

Irene was christened with the second name of Martha — after Da's mother's name. It is an eerie act of nature that she was given her granny's name as she had the actual nature that was closest to Da's — quick-tempered, bossy and 'never in the wrong'. I don't know if it was because of this similarity of character that he related to or that she had his own mother's name, but he frequently overlooked her traits when Ma and the rest of us would resent them, holding her actions and attitude against her when she'd ask for our help with anything. This is not to say that she didn't have compassion or selflessness or a sense of humour, but that I don't recall experiencing these till I was well into me teens — and even then, they were of a temporary nature. The fact that she had deep black hair whilst being surrounded by redheads rules out the old stereotype about a certain hair colour determining a fiery nature.

Snapshots of Irene are about arguments with Ma, owning a Slazenger tennis racket, taking command of the sitting room and studying non-stop before going off to university in Dublin. Of course, there was the army checkpoint story I shared with you earlier.

I only ever saw Ma cry twice; once at me granny's funeral, which was to be expected, and once after feeling the force of Irene's tongue. We had long left the Four Streets when me granny died, but still living there when Irene upset her.

Me and Paul had planned to go over the Tins but stayed by the house gable instead. We had had to abandon our game of 'keepie uppies' (for you non-football types, that's slang for keeping the ball off the ground by using your feet to continually kick the ball up in the air) when the old Derry rain had raised its ugly head again. We had only gone outside in the first place because we could feel some kind of tension inside the house. There was often a degree of tension, what with ten people crammed inside it. There had been silences and Ma and Da had been talking with their faces close together in the scullery. Outside, and especially over the Tins, was always a welcome escape from the house. The premature ending to the game was all the more frustrating as I was beating Paul too, with a top score of thirty-eight to his twenty-six after nine attempts. We had agreed the rules before we started (as always) — and we were to have ten attempts. The number of attempts or games or rounds or penalties were usually agreed and based on how much time we had and what the weather looked like. Checking the weather before going outside and estimating the forecast, became habitual by the time we turned five. Today, the clouded sky over the Donegal Mountains and the force of the wind didn't warrant too many attempts at 'keepie uppy' on this occasion. We knew the rain wouldn't be far from flying across the Atlantic, the mountains, the Creggan Estate, the Bogside, Foyle Street, the River Foyle, the railway line and ultimately the Tins and the Four Streets — always from the west. This competition (and many others) took place within the imaginary rectangle that was bordered on one side by the house gable wall and on one end by the garage door. There were no lines for the other side or end, so we had to be scrupulous in keeping to the imaginary lines. Although we were always fiercely competitive, we were also fair and honest when possible contentious decisions emerged. We also had an unspoken agreement that the 'other' could see better than the one who was actively playing or kicking at the time — almost like a referee's advantageous viewpoint over a player who would be focusing on the ball. Trust in the other was vital.

We got to nine goes each when the heavens opened and the cold drops from the now darkened sky put an end to our game. Although I had won the moral victory, it was not the same as winning the actual game. A game abandoned meant the result was void. It was always a relief to the losing player, in any game, when the game was abandoned owing to such things as rain or time being cut short by tea being ready or Da arriving home or sisters shouting for peace and quiet. But the losing player knew in their heart of hearts that they'd been beaten. The winning player also knew there was no point in trying to gloat as the void result deemed any such behaviour absolutely futile. There would be a 'defeated' silence following such abandoned games.

So it was with this silence that we ran back indoors, to be greeted by a different kind of silence in the hallway that seemed to emanate from the kitchen and the scullery. We had re-entered the tomb of tension and the uncomfortableness that we had earlier easily forgotten about once we'd got outside. I could feel me stomach churn and me mouth go instantly dry as there was no sign of Ma. I checked the backyard in case she'd been out rescuing clothes from the wet skies, but no, still no Ma. No Da, either. Neither me nor Paul spoke.

Then in what seemed like ages, we could hear muffled voices coming from upstairs — from our sisters' room. I knew that it was only Irene who was in. Then there were a rush of steps on the stairs and Ma came rushing into the scullery with tears in her eyes, with Da on her heels. I hadn't seen her tears before and could feel me own body tighten and me chest have a blockage of some kind, preventing me from breathing properly. I knew I couldn't speak either. I ran to the sofa where Paul had taken refuge, and sat beside him, the pair of us with our knees up to our chest. We were like two little puppies sitting scared but without really knowing why.

Despite the tears, Ma's blubbering voice could be heard.

"I can't take this any more. Did you hear the names she called me? She's got a hell of a temper and she didn't get it from me! I would never have spoken to me own mother the way she speaks to me."

Da didn't say a word — neither to collude or to chastise or even to comfort. His silence made it worse and only served to make Ma cry more. I had to really concentrate to get a sense of it all, but the individual words such as 'couldn't go', 'concert', 'camping', 'cruel', 'slapped' and 'your favourite' left me with enough to go on to add the padding to the story of events. Irene hadn't been allowed to go away with friends for the weekend to Ballybofey in Donegal. Ma's worries about her safety were paramount in her stating that Irene couldn't go. With any of the rest of us, Da would have stated the rules, but with Irene he would be different — he'd be much more passive. So it had been up to Ma to call the shots on this occasion, which provoked forty lashings from Irene's tongue and one slap across the face from her swinging right palm.

Da still said nothing.

Once there was enough wordage to go on, me and Paul retreated to the sitting room to piece together the storyboard and start our own amateur critique of the performance of the main protagonists.

"I can't believe she hit Ma!"

"Imagine hitting your own ma?"

"Just because she couldn't get her own way."

"Jesus!"

"They must have been rowing for ages."

"Why didn't Da do something?"

"If that had been us he would have murdered us!"

"He lets her off with murder."

"Why?"

"He always lets them [sisters] off with anything."

"And we just get whacked for looking at nothing!"

The rain was still coming down so we couldn't get out of the house. We couldn't go back into the kitchen either, especially as we knew that Da would be in a bad mood and would quickly take it out on us. So we resorted to the last resort, and pulled out the five-hundred piece jigsaw puzzle of the Houses of Parliament standing proudly on the side of the Thames. We kept it safely, on a large piece of hardboard that Da got from work, under the red settee. It had been easy to construct Big Ben, but the thousand-year-old brickwork that had similar spires and turrets stretching their arms up to the sky was much more challenging. Doing such focused activity is a great way to distract the brain from focusing on more chaotic thinking, so it allowed both of us to relax a bit and eventually exchange some dialogue about the jigsaw pieces. This was one of those few moments where competition wasn't allowed to reside

— it was all about teamwork. Before we knew it, Ma gave us a shout that tea was ready. Normality resumed. I don't recall any other obvious clashes between Ma and Irene after that but there was a tension between them that never really went away. Some things are just not tangible.

If Irene's short temper was a negative trait that allowed her to stand out from the rest of us, her education and learning prowess was definitely a positive one.

I had no real idea of the Derry school system and the status and possible 'advancement' of having a grammar school education, but was aware that it was clearly a big thing for parents if any of their beloved children passed the eleven-plus, and therefore had the golden ticket to go to such a one. Mina didn't manage that feat but Irene did. The grey blazer, trimmed with yellow and red and with the grammar school badge sitting proudly on the breast pocket, made Irene stand out as a cut above the rest. Whether the grammar school was a Protestant one or a Catholic one, social hierarchy was evident by the 'posh' blazers worn by its pupils — made of wool, weighing heavier and much more robust than your typical flimsy secondary school blazer. Saying that, I don't think the 'second rate' schools even had a blazer! There was Londonderry High School and Foyle College for the Protestant 'achievers' and St Columb's College and Thornhill College for the Catholic 'achievers'. Gender division was deemed necessary for a solid education to take place if you attended grammar, whereas there was no such ideology given to those attending schools outside of this system. Each of the Four Streets had a handful of houses with one or more of these success stories, with their blazers standing proudly on top of the educational pile. The wearers of these blazers clearly adopted an air of superiority; they knew the blazer could lead to all sorts of possibilities later in life, like university, career and wealth. The likes of me also knew of this, as well as of the alternate fate of a poor education, little or no qualifications, a low-paid job and a life in 'Troubled' Derry or its surrounding potholes of joblessness.

This superior attitude of the grammar school blazer wearer was nurtured by a chosen few from the Four Streets; no more so than by Irene. By the time me and Paul entered this world, this attitude had taken some shape but grammar school allowed it to be ungrained. Everyone felt the force of this attitude that would display itself via her bossiness, but the likes of two little boys (me and Paul) were easy pickings. It was also symbolised by her sitting on her 'rightful' throne — one of the large red armchairs in the sitting room.

This particular armchair was a couple of feet closer to the hearth and therefore closer to the most-sought-after electric fire; it also gave the one sitting in it a territorial view of the window and the street. Irene always felt the cold easily and therefore demanded this chair. As a little boy I would feel intimidated by her bossy voice and usually give in without too much of a fight. There would naturally be a sense of 'order' in any large family so giving in to one of me older sisters, was a regular thing anyway, though I did resent it as it stank of unfairness and inequality. More often than not, me and Paul would be relegated to the floor space and kneel on this whilst leaning on the settee to do homework, or even worse, concede to the floor space behind the settee and by the draughty door, away from the fire and only the carpeted floor to lean on. I knew my place in the family hierarchy. I guess on the bright side, it prepared me in some way for the inequality and unfairness that became rife in life — that's rife in all our lives. I was never shocked by such experiences later in life and therefore didn't get too upset, when it happened to me, but I would be greatly angered when I saw others experience unfairness or inequality.

I was no different to any kid when it came to doing something that was normally not possible because of rules and powerlessness. So I would occasionally sneak into the sitting room, put on the electric fire (but ONLY when Da wouldn't be able to detect that it had been on) and sit like the King of Ulster on Irene's red throne — wonderful!

Another sneaky thing that I would do that involved Irene was to hold and swing her precious tennis racquet. Tennis was not what it became by the nineties; a game that parents with enough spare cash could throw at to give their children *another* activity to fill up their out-of-school time on. By the time Henman and Murray came along to give the British media something patriotic to shout about (apart from the one-off moment of Virginia Wade), tennis became readily accessible to most kids. It wouldn't just be the hallowed green grass of Wimbledon that kids could dream of playing at, but also the multi-coloured hard courts and rusty-red clay courts across the globe that Sky batted across our forever-growing television screens. It wasn't just the tiny sports shop off the main high street that an expensive tennis racquet could be purchased in, but a whole range of massive sports stores in city centres, out-of-town retail outlets and online shops. Choice and accessibility became part of kids' lives in the nineties.

For me, tennis by the end of the sixties was Wimbledon on the BBC... and nothing else; whiter-than-white polo shirts, shorts, socks and even tennis shoes (trainers); no logo embroidered on shirts or socks or baseball caps; no grunting when hitting the ball; no challenging the umpire; no Cyclops to compensate for a line judge's limited naked human eye; no gym-pumped physiques; no bright green grass beaming from the TV screen — just a cloudy greyness colouring in-between the Daz-white straight lines. Then there was the soft, husky, eloquent tones of Dan Maskell, whispering the names of greats such as John Newcombe, Rod Laver and Margaret Court.

I never thought much about the racquets these stars used apart from ignorantly thinking they were not unlike the two that me and Paul possessed. Woolworths had anything and everything you could have wanted. We never had the opportunity or need to enter Temple's Sports Store on Carlisle Road as all our school sports clothes and school uniforms were purchased from Rutherford's — apart from football boots from Galloway's shoe shop on Ferryquay Street. Woolworths had our footballs, cricket bats and stumps and our tennis racquets. The stars' tennis racquets looked the same as ours and sounded the same as ours when they hit a tennis ball; so we thought no different.

Then one day when all me sisters were out of the house during the summer before Irene would leave for Trinity College in Dublin, I had a sneaky look in their bedroom. The room looked different to Ma and Da's that we slept in; it had two windows for starters, but it smelt different and seemed larger. There was nothing to look for specifically; I was just having a nose. Then tucked in the corner next to one of the windows and to the side of the 'modern' chest of drawers (not dark oak like in Ma and Da's room, but a lighter teak colour), there it was; a strange wooden contraption with a tennis racquet stuck in it.

I lifted it and immediately realised that it was a hell of a lot heavier than my racquet. There was no Woolworths sticker on the handle, but the name Slazenger. I knew it was a famous name and therefore an expensive one from the sports shop. I also realised that this was like the Wimbledon players' racquets. It took a while before I worked out that the square wooden frame that the racquet was in was to protect it and keep the round frame of the racquet intact. Wow, I thought, this was amazing. The square frame had a spring-like catch that was really tricky to undo (was this Irene's idea of keeping us boys away from it I thought) but eventually I unclipped it and was able to slip out the racquet from its place of imprisonment. I caressed every inch of its frame, every inch of its taught strings. The strings were nothing like the floppy ones on me own racquet, which would part like the Red Sea every time you'd hit the ball a good whack and I would then have to spend ages trying to straighten them up and attempt to create perfectly even gaps between them. Nothing bothered me more than to look at wonky and angled strings. It would annoy Paul like hell when I would spend time fixing them during our own 'Wimbledon' finals, but I just couldn't concentrate if there were huge gaps. I'd only become really self-critical if I played a wonky shot because I hadn't bothered to straighten strings! I didn't see this as compulsive behaviour; more about having the patience to do something simple in order to give the intended hit its best shot. The competitive ingredient was in there too, of course.

I still often think that sometimes taking a few seconds or even minutes to help to bring about a positive outcome is worth doing. So if I get into the car and realise I've forgotten to bring something with me, I never think 'Aw no, I can't be bothered' and leave it;

I'll spend those few seconds to go back. I guess, I often think that we see a small task as something much greater than it actually is. Take a moment to think about this the next time you forget something!

Anyway, I held Irene's wonder racquet and turned it over and over in me hands to see and feel the strapping of the handle covering. It was so heavy I could barely swing it about as I tried to emulate Rod Laver. He made it look so easy, yet me own arm buckled under the weight as I swung it round. I was better at the double-handed back swing as I could use both arms. I played shot after shot on the Number One court as I stood at the bottom of the double bed that Hazel and Val shared, returning Newcombe's serve with devastating force as he ran to the net, only to have me pass him down the lines. I would win point after point after point. It wasn't long before I raised the silver shield with me name engraved on the outer circle — 'Sid Kennedy, Champion 1969'. The photographers brightly flashed their cameras, matched only by me champion-beaming grin.

I had no idea how long I had been on 'court', but I then heard footsteps on the stairs — it was Ma. She panicked to see me with Irene's racquet and quickly ordered me to put it back where I'd got it, as she would soon be back home. The last thing Ma wanted was another tempered scene in the house, so she told me to get a move on and put it back and headed back downstairs. The only thing was, she didn't know that it had come out of a strange wooden contraption. If it had been difficult to get it out of this square frame, it was surely impossible to get it back in. I got half of it in but I couldn't open the frame wide enough to get it all in. It needed an adult's strong hands. Ma's would have done the job but if she'd seen the bigger picture, she would have seen the bigger hole I'd dug for meself. This then would have led to a bigger scolding for me, and probably the ultimate threat, "wait till your da gets home". Me mind was whirling with thoughts of Irene shouting at me, Ma shouting at me and Da shouting at me. The more I thought about the shouting, the more I panicked.

Oh no, there's the front door.

I quickly shoved it back in its resting place and disappeared from the scene of the crime. Me heart was all over the place and me head was chaotic. By the time Ma called that tea was ready I had calmed down. The house seemed normal… phew! I then forgot all about it.

About a week later I was watching *Marine Boy* — it was Saturday morning and I loved *Marine Boy* with his superpowers to deal with the baddies of the seas. Me and Paul were as fixated as ever with his swimming through the sea like a dolphin, and his cloak flowing behind him like a magic carpet. Everything he did seemed like magic and his movements were effortless. Like any child needing to escape the tensions of the real world, inside and outside of the house, having TV characters like Marine Boy and his underwater escapades and adventures, was pure joy. Stories were typically about baddies doing bad stuff like Spanish pirates raiding all the oysters and stealing the sparkling white pearls out of greed, or Russian sailors dumping their engine oil waste on the Great Barrier Reef. These baddies looked obviously evil to me, with their mean faces, deeply lined frowns, snarling black-gapped teeth, big fat fists and growling huge mouths. As scary as they were, at least I'd be able to recognise them. That's what made the whole Protestant/Catholic so-called hatred thing all the more difficult to comprehend. I played games with Protestant and Catholic friends — some looked less trustworthy than others but with possibly similar features regardless of religious persuasion. How could one person be labelled a baddie based on something that wasn't distinguishably identifiable? Playmates were usually only distinguishable by features that said more about their economic background or personality than anything else — except on a Sunday (I'll come to that later). So that meant everyone was potentially a suspect of baddie behaviour and baddie actions at first glance. Marine Boy had it easy — baddies were transparent, easy to spot and deserved whatever comeuppance they were dished out.

I didn't even notice Irene come into the kitchen as my eyes were bobbing up and down in motion with Marine Boy, parting the sky-blue waters on the back of his dolphin.

"Who's been in our room and messing around with

my good tennis racquet?"

My four older sisters all had a sharp tongue when they wanted to thrash you with it, but Irene's was an octave and a few decibels higher than the other three. It also had an edge as cutting as Zorro's blade. I felt the blade cut through my world of *Marine Boy* — Paul's trembling body movement reflected a similar form of his world being brutally sliced.

We turned in tandem as only twins could do, to witness Irene standing there with the racquet in her right hand, but with her body slightly lurched forward like a Halloween witch ready to poke a cherub-faced wain with her long and crooked nails. Irene was right-handed and I'd seen her swing the racquet with it before with some ferocity. I feared getting a whack with it, with the square frame still half attached. I'm sure Paul's thoughts were of a similar ilk. Paul often looked guilty in these occasions. I didn't consciously aim for him to get the blame, but I decided to play nonchalantly innocent in true Dennis the Menace style. Innocent till proven guilty was always a good starting point of Dennis. I'd perfected it with a vacant expression that gave no hint of emotion, feeling or thought. Da's blame-questioning served to fine tune such an expression as any sign of guilt would result in an instant whack. He didn't do the innocent till proved guilty rhetoric.

"Which one of you was it?" Irene probed.

Silence. Motionless. Fear.

"It was you, Sid, I know it was. You're always up

143

to something. Go on admit it." She was looking for a confession, as she always did. Not that the situation or potential blame or scolding would get any worse, just that she wanted to be proven right. She loved logic, reason and a dénouement. She would then relish the guilty party experiencing some degree of public humiliation and shame.

I decided that silence was the worse option of two, so I piped up:

"How d'ye know that somebody was messing with it?" I sounded confident, but was far from it. I usually found that speaking was a good distraction from the overwhelming feelings of fear or sadness that silence permitted — but this was only successful if the voice didn't give away these feelings.

"See, the frame is only half on." She lurched even further forward. Paul shook, but I stood firm.

"Maybe it slipped off by itself," I reasoned.

"Don't get smart with me," she burst, and poked me twice with the overhanging part of the wooden frame. I let on it hurt more than it did — Cato's philosophy had its moments, but now wasn't one of them. I knew that Irene wouldn't want to inflict too much pain, just enough to let off some of her steam.

"Leave my belongings alone," she snapped as she turned and went upstairs.

Ma poked her head round the scullery door frame just in time to see me smirk. Her scowl quickly erased what was left of it. Her right forefinger rose up in front of her and was shaken from side to side, before returning to her cooking. She didn't need words, but the humiliation was keenly felt. *Marine Boy* was still on, thank god, though his effortless underwater swimming contrasted with me own breathing. By the time the theme tune signalled the end of the episode, me stomach had settled and I forgot about Irene and her posh Slazenger tennis racquet with its contraption-of-a-frame.

It was about six years later that I recalled this incident again when I had taken up tennis at school and thought I was the new Bjorn Borg. Irene had been home during the hot summer of '76 and surprisingly challenged me to a game of tennis at the old courts at Altnagelvin Hospital. As usual I was seen in her eyes as one of the wee twin boys, who had not really grown up. I was pure mincemeat and a bit of practise for her. I played with my heart and soul, driven on by the memory of being poked by THAT racquet and THAT frame. Winning 6-0, 6-0 was utter joy. As we walked the ten minutes back to the house in reverent silence, I gave focus to my joy, and she in turn, gave focus to her feelings — possibly humiliation.

# Chapter 8
# Robin, the Firstborn Son

Defeating and humiliating me older brother Robin in tennis, or anything else for that matter was never going to happen, and never did. He was always just too big, too strong and too proud to give me even a sniff of a chance when it came to football. He didn't get the chance to entertain the grammar school sports of tennis or golf or hockey; it was all secondary modern sport with him at Clondermot — which was football. A social divide and a belief system nearly always started for us in education after primary. Irene was sandwiched between him and Mina in terms of the educational system that determined their lives thereafter. Being the sandwich filler made her feel even more special, even more middle class and even more superior. It also made their relationships more intense and more fraught. Robin didn't really relate to either of his elder sisters, purely because they were girls. He didn't relate to Mina because she was four years older and only shared one year at secondary with him, and he didn't relate to Irene once she moved on to the grammar school. He was Ma's first son so he had a special attention that the two girls didn't get. Even Da in his own fatherly way had a bit of a bond that he never attempted to have with his two daughters. Although, as I said earlier, he did have a connection with Irene that no one understood.

Football, of course, ran through me own veins too, so there was something I had in common with Robin, but the age gap of seven years meant he left me and Paul behind as he headed out to play footy with the boys his own age. Only occasionally he would take us two on in the backyard but he merely toyed with us and didn't hold back in his tackles either — often inflicting bruises on our skinny shins with his black brogues. He idolised Derek Duggan, the big Northern Ireland and Wolverhampton Wanderers centre forward. I could tell he wanted to be like him by the physical way he played. Moaning about his strong-man attitude would always bring out the bog-standard response, "It'll harden you up!" He was, of course, right, as I would establish the same physicality when out with me friends and especially on long summer nights when us wee boys were allowed special dispensation to play with the big boys in twenty-a-side games. These games were brilliant, and if I got to play on Robin's team, even better. One particular game stands out.

I remember it was the first week of July and all the schools in Derry had just finished for a great eight weeks of nothingness. Unknown to us, it was also the beginning of the last July of relative peace in Derry, as four months later the social and political divide raised its tumultuous head and the first Civil Rights march organised by the Northern Ireland Civil Rights Association took place in Derry — and the Troubles truly began.

Robin might have been aware of the significant religious tensions in the Four Streets, but I wasn't. He was aware of the Battle of the Boyne and the Easter Rising, the UDA and the IRA — I was just aware that Protestants did some things differently to Catholics; Protestants wore their Sunday 'best' to church, prayed to God, supported Glasgow Rangers, waved the Union Jack, didn't play out on Sundays, often had smaller families, whilst Catholics wore their everyday clothes to chapel, prayed to the Virgin Mary or the Pope, supported Glasgow Celtic, waved the Tricolour, played sport on Sundays and could have families as big as twenty.

The twenty-a-side teams had a mixture of players: Protestants, Catholics, six-year-olds, twenty-year-olds, long-haired, bald, bearded, shaven, too young to have facial hair, had no criminal record, had been to borstal, could use both feet to kick the ball, had two left feet, those who could control the ball and those who couldn't. The seagulls who flew above on their missions from the tops of sheds of the Four Streets to across the Tins and over the River Foyle, and back, must have thought it looked like their ancestors' early days of rugby football that was played on the streets of Rugby; had two sides with multiple numbers of players and was a mass frenzy of mayhem.

The Four Streets' pitch was the tarmac bit of road that stretched from the middle of the road at the bottom of York Street, along the gable of the bottom house and ended where the back lane behind it met the back wall of the house behind *it*, at the foot of Florence Street — all of forty yards. The goal at the Florence Street end was easy to determine as the back wall of its bottom house extended further into the road, making the road narrower between the railway sleeper wall and the house, and therefore the perfect width for a goal. The goal at the York Street end needed one post made from a boulder retrieved from the Tins placed in the middle of the road, whilst the sleeper wall acted as the other post. If the pitch had been dampened by rain, which was often the case, a line was drawn by sand that had been dumped over the Tins, to mark the goal line. If the pitch was dry, which it was on this July night in 1968, then a line was drawn by plasterboard chalk that had also been retrieved from over the Tins. Having a goal line didn't eliminate arguments about whether the ball had completely crossed it, but it gave some kind of guideline that reduced the ferocity of fracas between players, that could ensue from a 'goal line clearance' or goalie save.

The team captains this particular night were Robin and his mate Gregory. So in keeping with tradition, the rest of the players lined up along the railway sleeper wall waiting to be picked — the line almost ran the length of the pitch. Me, Paul, Billy and Shane stood on the end at the bottom of York Street. We knew we would be the last to be picked as we were the youngest and by far the smallest. We weren't always guaranteed to play, and it was left to the big boys to decide if there were too many players to allow us to play or not. If Robin was there, we had a better chance as he'd always say, "Och, sure they won't do any harm", but if he wasn't playing then some of the big boys would tell us to clear off as we'd only get hurt. What they really meant was that they wanted to be able to play hard and not take it easy if the likes of me or Paul had the ball. Me and Shane were on Robin's side which meant that we would at least have one of the big boys pass the ball to us. I don't blame the bigger boys of ignoring wee boys like me and not passing the ball when I was available for a pass — I was just happy to be on the pitch. I usually had a kick of the ball by default, when the ball would ricochet off someone's anatomy and come to me. As there were so many players on the pitch it was impossible for good passing movements or lengthy dribbles to happen as tackles would fly in from all directions once you had possession of the dirty-white ball that was either lacking air and soft and heavy to kick, or over-pumped, hard as concrete and swirled around in the wind. Tonight, the ball was the latter, so I knew that skill levels would be low and that there was a greater chance of getting touches of the ball by pure chance. The game was typically competitive and the score typically ebbed and flowed like a baby's cradle being rocked by a granny's toe. I had a couple of touches that went to one of me own players, but got a rollicking from Robin and the whole team after I gave the ball away that led to the equaliser — the score was now 19-19. The games never started off with an agreed winning score, like having the winning team being the first to ten; they were always determined during the match by the two captains. This looseness of rules wouldn't have happened in the Kennedy house as they were always set out before a game started — clarity of rules was the ultimate leveller. The weather, the natural light, the calls by parents for their offspring to come in for bed, the condition of the ball and whether the ball couldn't be retrieved from someone's backyard, were all factors that led to the end of the match being determined. Tonight's game was a close affair and so eventually Robin (who had scored a hat-trick) and Gregory agreed that when the scores were 17-16 to us, the winners would be the first to twenty. Having felt I let Robin and the whole team down by being responsible for the opposition's equaliser, I was determined to make amends and gain Robin's respect. So I hung around near the opposition's goal. Then Robin barged past two players just like Derek Duggan, but I could see two more quickly descending on him to make a tackle. I was screaming for it. He looked over at my direction. Earlier in the game he might have passed it to me but the stakes were too high so instead he belted the ball from ten yards out. The ball swirled in the air. Pete Mulcahy got his left knee down to save it and it spun off Jimmy Watson's shin and bobbled to me but on my weaker foot, my left. I was only one yard from the goal. I couldn't trust the ball enough or trust meself enough to try and control the ball and get it unto me right foot, so I just swung me left foot instinctively instead, and in it went — the winner! I was Georgie Best personified and duly did his trademark pose of one arm in the air. I could hear the roar of me team mates — they didn't care who scored; their minds were on winning. Robin didn't run over to me and lift me up on his shoulders as if I was Bobby Moore at the World Cup. I didn't need him to — his beaming smile was all that I needed to see. I was tonight's hero. Pride was restored. It was the only moment that I felt Robin's respect but it warmed me body with satisfaction nevertheless.

Robin had his own sense of what respect meant, and it wasn't going to rest on his wee brother, but rightfully so, on his peers, boys his own age. This was no more demonstrated than days leading up to the traditional bonfire burning a couple of years after me football heroics. There were two such occasions that were marked by the Protestant community during the summer months. They were both called 'The Twelfth' — one in July and one in August, and both marked Protestant battle wins over Catholics, hundreds of years before. Well, the Protestants saw it that way, as the filtered and partisan history (as is always the case in the eye of any history writer) that they adhered to, portrayed Catholics as the perpetrator and oppressor, and

152

Protestants as the minority and defender of their land, heritage and faith. The Orangemen chant of "No Surrender" that Dr Ian Paisley loved to shout from the television screen and into our kitchens, reflected this mentality; one that conveyed Protestants as the battle-hardened underdog who had resilience and true grit to see off all enemies. There are always two sides to a story, of course.

The July Twelfth was to commemorate the Battle of the Boyne win where the disposed Catholic King James' army was defeated by the newly acceded Protestant Prince William of Orange's (he was Dutch!) army at the River Boyne in Ireland. This battle was celebrated by Orangemen across the whole of Northern Ireland, a few pockets in the Republic of Ireland, Scotland and beyond. The fact that both armies were made up of men from a range of countries across Europe, who were desperate to earn a living and had no real allegiance to either leader, apart from the fact that they were the ones paying their wages, is lost on the Protestant psyche. Although the anniversary celebration was about giving the Protestant community the opportunity to 'remember' past victories, in reality it was about showing 'two fingers' to Catholics in as loud a fashion as possible. The Orange Order lodge would march along the streets in a religiously civil fashion, but each one would be immediately followed by a band (pipe, flute or accordion) that played Orange tunes accompanied by the loud beating of deafening drums.

The decibel pitch would rise when the marches passed any nearby Catholic-dominated street or area of housing to prove the mantra of 'No Surrender'.

The August Twelfth parade was a similar show of Protestant culture and belief, but there was only one parade — it took place in Derry and was dubbed the Apprentice Boys Parade. This date was to commemorate another victory of Protestants over Catholics — this time by the defending of Derry's walled city from King James' Catholic ships that sat on the city's River Foyle and bombarded its walls with heavy cannon fire. The story states that it was a number of Protestant apprentices from within the city who closed its gates and which led to a one-hundred-and-five-day-long siege — and the later founding of the Apprentice Boys of Derry Society. So, on 12th August each year, thousands of Protestants would flock to me home city and create as much noise as possible as a show of strength and intimidation. It was a day when all me Catholic friends would either stay in their homes or disappear across the border to relatives for a couple of days — such was the emergence of fear.

It is much easier to have a simple version of war where victory, liberation and rule was gained in a battle between *us* Protestants and *them* Catholics. I always thought it was odd that the history curriculum in Protestant schools (like the ones I went to) never covered Irish history, never covered the historical dimensions between the two communities who lived across the Four Streets, never covered the relationship between England and Ireland, and therefore never allowed a different view to the one commonly held in Protestant homes. The history that was passed down to Protestant generations was the one that came from the lips of parents to their offspring, from the marches on the streets, from the practising of Orange tunes in Orange Halls and the burning of bonfires on the eve of each Twelfth; it didn't come from textbooks that made us read or write an essay on. It took me years to find out that there was another story to read, to tell, to believe, to play, to embrace — one that me Catholic friends knew about and had been taught to them in their own schools. It seems strange now to reflect that they never talked about their 'own' view of history. One too, that I suspect Ma and Da knew about too but chose not to tell me about — just like all the other Protestant mas and das.

As with every other aspect of the Troubles and the participants in it, symbolism, as a sign of strength, territory and rule, was a huge part of both Protestant and Catholic cultures. Flags and colours were keen benefactors of such symbolism; Protestants wouldn't wear green with yellow and Catholics wouldn't wear blue with red and this would mean representing the 'enemy'. Another act of symbolism was the burning of bonfires late into the summer night. So, on the 11th Night (in July and August), bonfires would be lit across the province. The bonfires would bring light to the fading summer skies, but more importantly would be an aperitif to the following day's marches and parades across villages, towns and cities. Although the July 11th night was revered, it was the August 11th night that had special meaning to the Protestants in Derry. Me brother, Robin, was typical of his generation, where preparing for this bonfire had greater meaning to the one on the previous month. The bonfire in August 1970 had even greater significance for him.

The Troubles had well and truly started: the streets of Derry's Bogside area became the new battlefields of differing ethno-nationalism, the British troops had been deployed, shootings and bombings became the new culture across the province, and fear swept through every street, every home, every bedroom and through the veins of every of the Troubles' inhabitants.

The building for the August bonfire began a mere few days after the ashes of the July's bonfire had gone cold. It seemed irreverent to start preparation for one commemoration before the acknowledgement of the previous commemoration had seen its natural course. So, Robin with his mates began the customary collecting of fuel for the August 11th night bonfire once the 'orange' psyche moved from celebrating the July battle to celebrating the August one.

More timber, tyres (that just gave out thick black smoke when burning), sleepers, furniture, bed frames, picture frames, fences and anything that remotely looked as if it might burn (made from metal or plastic came into this category), was thrown in the heap close to the ashes from the July's bonfire — ready for the older boys like Robin to assemble 'professionally'. They were now the experienced ones who had learned from their elders before them, the way a good bonfire should be built for maximum effect. The one other crucial consideration was to construct the bonfire in such a way that it had a hollow space in the middle for a couple of crouched bodies. This was so that a level of security could take place to avoid the would-be enemy (Catholics) to set it alight prematurely. Boys of all ages would volunteer to 'keep dick' (act as Apache scouts) from dawn till a short time past dusk. It was deemed an honour to be chosen as one of the volunteers as it provided street credit of huge proportions. More often than not though, it was teenage boys who got the nod to 'keep dick', or who would demonstrate their right in the street pecking order of masculinity and claim the honourable position. The odd, briefly contested fist fight would take place when testing of the pecking order emerged. A couple of well-aimed punches usually ended such a contest — rematches were rare. Just like all male hierarchical social structures, the pecking order would be challenged regularly. In the ape world, this might be during the annual mating season, in the urban street world, it was during the 'Marching season' — named to mark the Protestant annual marches during the months of July and August. I wasn't one for getting involved in street hierarchies; I didn't like fighting for real and the thought of violence made me feel sick. Watching others fight and see blood spilled from noses and mouths was enough to turn me stomach. Being a spectator was sickening enough at times, so getting in the ring was a definite No. Added to that, I knew that Da didn't believe in street fights and violence. So if I ever I were to get dragged into a fight, the hassle, telling-off and possible slap from Da was deterrent enough. Not surprisingly then, I only had fleeting moments of sitting inside the bonfire's hollow. It was a good feeling to not feel I missed out on something most of me friends would brag about and not be slagged that I was a scaredy-cat. It was clearly a rite of passage that we all had to experience, but one that I would swear blind to Ma and Da that I never did. Ma would constantly tell me and Paul to keep away from the bonfire but her busy schedule of housewife and being a ma didn't allow her time to 'keep dick' herself — she left that to Da and Da's 'eyes' — the nosy neighbours who fed him crumbs from the loaf of bad behaviour.

Collecting the bonfire's fuel was something Ma also frowned at but she didn't put her foot down on me and Paul rummaging around the Tins or dragging the drawers from some old chest of drawers, or broken lampshade that had been left out on the back lanes by someone who knew that it'd be collected by us bonfire foot soldiers. Ma would deem this as not doing any harm. However, I would make sure that I didn't have any role in cutting or dragging branches off trees from the nearby St Columb's Park, which became the norm if the big boys thought that fuel supplies were low. The fuel for July's fire was plentiful as it had been almost a year since people in the Four Streets had done any meaningful spring-cleaning and had the opportunity to get rid of their rubbish, but fuel for August's fire would ultimately, be in short supply. Hence, the urge to cut down parts of trees from the park that was only a few hundred yards away, along the railway line; it was probably the potential danger of walking along the railway tracks that bothered Ma more than about the cutting of trees for the bonfire. August's bonfire sure had a luscious green colour to it when it was fully erected. The irony of the nationalist colour green shouldn't be lost here!

"The bonfire. The bonfire."

I was woken up to Robin's roar as he came out of his bedroom at the bottom of the lower landing and bolted down the stairs, out through the vestibule door, the front door and over the Tins. Da was up quickly as usual but didn't get too flustered by the unusual voice alarm raised by Robin. Me and Paul waited till he could be heard going down the stairs before scuttling out of the bedroom down to Robin's room. Da would only have told us to stay in our beds if he'd seen us. I was rarely in Robin's room. It was uninviting with its cold, squared-shaped lino of blues and greens that wouldn't have looked out of place in a nineties bathroom! The lino looked like a huge expanse of sea which was uninterrupted by any island of mat to protect feet from its coldness. There was a single bed behind the door against the wall and a solitary teak-coloured wardrobe that took central position against the wall facing you as you entered. Why was it that wardrobes took the regal role in our bedrooms? They were the bits of furniture that dominated over any other, no matter how brightly coloured or fanciful they might have been. They were always pretty large in breadth and height. They also contained the most interesting of our possessions; shoes, trousers, shirts, games, uniforms, sports gear, bible-class certificates, cups, medals, school books, comics and magazines. Robin's wardrobe had the kudos of a sleeping bag that he used for Scout camping expeditions at Portrush or mates' expeditions on the beach at Fahan or Buncrana in Donegal. The fact that it was green and yellow was another irony. None of me sisters owned one, and I didn't know of anyone else who owned one either. I wouldn't dare take it out of its green bag for fear of not getting it back in — a challenge that can still haunt any would-be camper today, despite the easy-to-fold and flexible, nylon-based sleeping bags that can be pushed and shoved into their waterproof cocoon. Robin's heavy, goose-feathered bag was less flexible and had to be folded to a precision fit for the army, in order to fit snuggly into its heavy cotton casing. However, before Robin would go 'camping', he would allow me and Paul to have a go at folding it and trying to fit it into its casing. I remember spreading it full length in the quiet sitting room and listening to his instructions:

"Fold the sides inwards so that the ends meet in the middle. Use your hands to push out the air that's inside. Repeat so that the bag is about twenty inches wide. Roll it up starting from the unopened end. Push the bag into the floor as hard as possible and keep the bag as tight as possible so that the air disappears out of the open end. Keep your knee on top of the rolled bag to stop any loosening or unravelling, and use the two cotton ties to tie it up tightly. Put it into the green cotton case that is just like a thin duffle bag."

It was impossible to do! Me hands were too small and not strong enough to produce the pressure needed to get rid of the air and to keep the whole bag tight enough to fit into the case. Just when I thought I'd managed the 'perfect' roll up, the bag would move ever so slightly, but slightly enough so that the tightness needed was jeopardised and eventually lost. It didn't help either that the bag stank of body odour and earthiness, and that these pungent smells would escape from within, every time it was squeezed. When I eventually was allowed to use the sleeping bag a couple of years later, I slept in it with pride, and felt like a man. The fact that Ma had thoroughly washed it with Daz helped!

When me and Paul ran into Robin's room, it was about four o'clock in the morning — a Saturday. Saturday 9th August, two days before the eleventh night and the lighting of the bonfire to celebrate the Apprentice Boys' closing of the city's gates. The bonfire had taken shape and was virtually complete. Only a few odd bits of wood would be added now. The older boys keeping dick had gone home to their beds five hours earlier, after a few cans of Harp to set them on their way. The sun had been up two hours earlier. Robin's curtains were wide open and blowing in the summer morning breeze that ushered through the open window. Robin had opened it wide to get a good look at what he'd seen through the glass. Me and Paul now looked out to see smoke coming from the bonfire, but no flames. We couldn't see anyone, not even Robin. Da was standing by the sleepers, peering over them with much intensity. Where was Robin? Ma had now joined us but me sisters had gone back to bed once they found out it was "just the bonfire". Me sisters never understood the primitive man in us boys needing to build fires. They were happy to watch from a distance when it was lit, but never got involved in the carrying of fuel, of keeping dick and the tension of keeping it 'safe' till lighting time.

Then Robin appeared from the bonfire's hole-of-a-doorway, his face, arms and upper body blackened from the smoke. He'd taken off his T-shirt to put out the flames that were growing inside, but hadn't spread through the outer walls for us to see. He then used his T-shirt to batter out any small flame that thought of breathing more deeply. The smoke got less and less as

162

we watched. No one spoke, not even Ma. It was like watching a scene from the Wild West when Commanche braves had tried to burn the 7th Cavalry Corp's tents on a raid before the big battle the next day. Eventually, Robin stood and turned to us watching and raised both his arms. He looked more like a Commanche than a Cavalry Colonel, but it was clear that he was victorious. He was clearly the hero. His street credit grew enormously amongst his peers. He was the new Apprentice Boy who had seen off the Catholic assailants. I'm not sure that Ma saw it quite like that. Fear of him coming to harm when inside the bonfire put paid to any thoughts of medals or accolades.

There were many suspicions on who had attempted to burn the bonfire prematurely, but over the weeks, Kevin Burns' name was pure dirt. His absence in the Four Streets for months after, seemed to only prove his guilt. It all served to heighten security for both summer bonfires for as long as the Tins remained as their place of birth, life and death.

# Chapter 9
# Hazel, the Fourth Born

I didn't witness any similar acts of heroinism with the next sibling in line, Hazel. I also didn't have any experience of playing sport with her either — her preference for hockey rather than football saw to that. Hockey was a typical grammar school sport, one that never entered the gates of the lower echelons of my secondary modern school. The mystery of what we don't know can often lead us to wondering what the subject is all about; it was the same for me about hockey. I wondered how it was played, how many players were on the pitch, what positions they played and how goals were scored. I'd seen the shape of the hurling stick when watching the TV in Donegal, with its axe-like head, but the shape of Hazel's hockey stick was very different. It was more like a golf club to me than a hurling stick, with its short, curved, but thick, head. They both posed lethal weapons on the pitch, though the hurling stick seemed more dangerous to the head as it was swung high in the air, whereas the hockey stick seemed more a threat to shins and ankles as the ball was usually hit on the ground. I'd see Hazel head off to school with her hockey stick and black, ankle-length rubber boots, but had no idea of the game itself — it was never televised. It wasn't an Olympic sport in the sixties or seventies, so I didn't get a glimpse of it on the box. However, there was one day when what happened after a game at school was more significant than the game itself.

BOOM... BOOM... BOOM!

The TV picture went fuzzy, came back, went fuzzy again, came back, went fuzzy the third time, and came back. *Blue Peter* was on and Ma had set the table. Tea of fried mince, fried sausage and fried potato was almost ready — I could always tell by the strength of the smell of the re-used lard that tea was near being put on the plates. The smell was strong to begin with, but with the added smells of the processed meat and the spuds, the pungent lard smell had meandered its way into me throat, lungs and up me nose!

"Oh, god, what's that now?" Ma screamed from the scullery doorway. "Hazel's still not home from school yet, and there's three bombs just gone off. They're not far away either, did ye see how the windows rattled? I thought they were goin' te blow in with the third bang. Shocking."

"The telly's gone off, Ma, and *Blue Peter*'s on," I murmured.

"Will ye give over 'bout the telly and bleedin' *Blue Peter*. Hazel's not back yet and there's three bombs have gone off. She could be caught up in them."

I'd heard that nervous tone of Ma's loads of times

165

when something like this had happened. I too felt my insides jump up and down a bit. The shock of the Booms and the deathly rattling of the glass windows in their sash frames always meant that it took ages for me feeble body to settle down. I couldn't understand what this 'war' of bombing, shooting, killing, petrol-bombing, rioting and knee-capping was all about. I just knew that the repercussions on all our lives was devastating and irreparable. I knew too that Ma would be a bag of nerves till Hazel got back in safely — she'd been playing hockey after school and therefore would be later home than normal. I knew too that this 'bag of nerves' would go on and on and on in a monologue of fear and worry, whilst she fantasised what each bomb was, where it happened, what was bombed and if Hazel had got on the bus home before they went off. Her Greek tragedy chorus would be on repeat. It was like listening to the sequence of forty-five single records that could be stacked on the record player and would drop down one at a time till they all played their hearts out. The dropping of one after another was inevitable after the first one dropped — only the intervention of a jam of some sort halted their fate. With Ma though, the intense background music might have varied slightly, but her anxious voice would be the same and the lyrics echoing fear and dread would be more or less the same too. There would be no way me insides could settle properly with that music in my ears.

The telly came back on, but Da quickly switched it

off and shouted:

"Don't put it back on, I'm goin' to put news on the radio!"

This too was a familiar song and the anxious, tense dread of his lyrics played a perfect duet with Ma's. I could then hear the perfect orchestral accompaniment of the puttering and familiar sound of the investigative helicopters flying out of the navy base a hundred yards away. The musical canon was complete. Before Da put the radio on, which I knew would mean utter silence, even from Ma, he went outside to see what he could see. Nobody went with him as it was now dark, but he loved these lone scouting missions and then returning to give his sermon on the kitchen mount, according to Saint Da — pure scriptures.

When bombs had gone off during daylight, Da would have been outside for ages, having a good look over the Tins, across the railway lines and across the River Foyle, trying to figure out what was happening. He would also have been gossiping with neighbours who too would have been guessing and building pictures and stories to retell over and over again, till some official news on the telly or on the radio or in the *Belfast Telegraph* gave the 'true' account of the latest battle of this war. As it was dark, Da was back in a few minutes,

"The helicopters are flying around Foyle Street and I can see smoke. There's sirens and blue flashing lights everywhere, but it's difficult to see any fires cos it's dark. Let's see what's on the radio."

How the transmitting of news has changed over the decades. By the second decade of the millennium, any terrorist attack is on Facebook and online news forums within seconds of something happening — often accompanied by mobile phone footage. Politicians are venting their anger with politically correct (usually) rhetoric on Twitter before emergency services have dealt with a situation. This is now the norm. However, back in the early seventies, news of any incidents during the Troubles were miraculously transmitted to the masses at an incredible speed via the radio. Some people's jobs at BBC Radio Ulster must have been purely about waiting for an act of terror to take place so that bulletins could crudely interrupt a programme (which happened regularly) to give listeners a dose of death and destruction.

Da knew this daily interruption and seemed to love hearing of such incidents so he could retell to himself or to anyone interested enough to listen. When he was at work, he didn't have the opportunity to hear instant news, and must have found this really frustrating. At home, he was like an army comms unit in the middle of the Vietnamese jungle with constant radio contact with HQ to get updates on enemy movements and positions of fellow Marines. If the signal was dodgy, he'd doggedly persevere and find a location in the house or a position for the aerial where reception was good enough to fill his head with graphic updates of bombings and killings... and the rest of any disturbing detail. What was worse, was a programme on the telly being interrupted and a news bulletin being announced. Even though the bulletin might only have lasted for twenty seconds, the fallout was longer-lasting as the domino effect took place. BBC One was then substituted by its UTV cousin and then by its second cousin, BBC Radio Ulster, until Da had his head full of enough detail of the latest sectarian incident. This occasion was no different.

Radio Foyle didn't exist in those days, so it was down to Radio Ulster to keep us posted of recent sectarian events. Brendan Dooley was the presenter — he would remind us, as DJs do all the time, of who was doing the radio shift at that present moment. He did a bit of the usual blathering about shopping habits and was joined by the usual callers who were keen to tell us what they were hoping to buy their loved ones for Christmas. It was the last week in November and shops had just started decorating their shop fronts and filling their shelves with box gifts of shampoo and bath salts, woolly hats and matching gloves, and children's toys such as Compendium of Games and Monopoly. Christmas festivities started much later in those days, unlike today when it now starts in late August — and before families empty their suitcases after their holiday in the sun, and while their brown bodies still reflect the hours spent worshipping it.

Dooley played a few songs (too early for Christmas songs), one by Philomena Begley, one by Tom Jones and one by Elvis, interjected by sarcasm and cynicism of Woolworths' and Stewarts' retail strategy. All of us sat mute as Da always demanded that we adhered to a church silence when the news was on the telly or the radio, or in this case, when he was *waiting* for the news to come on. Even Ma had put tea on hold so as not to interrupt the 'service'. Nevertheless, it seemed a lifetime and a half before Da got his wish. Dooley unlovingly interrupted Elvis' 'An American Trilogy' and abruptly announced that there would be a newsflash, and that he was transferring the listeners to the news studio.

"Three car bombs have gone off in Londonderry city centre within the last half an hour. The IRA have claimed responsibility. No further details are known at this point, but security services have arrived on the scene."

The newsreader had done his job — confirmed what we had all suspected in the first place — that there had been bombs 'over the town'; that's what we called the main and historical part of Derry, across the River Foyle from where we were, on the Waterside.

"Oh, dear," said Dooley, before Da did his own bit of crude interrupting and switched the wireless off. It would have been a blessing to have heard the next song or two, if only to ease the tension in the room, but Da wasn't one for sentiment or compassion at times like this. His thirst for deathly and depressing detail superseded any desire for positivity or quiet reflection.

Da checked the clock on the mantelpiece; it was twenty-five to six. He quickly switched the telly back on for the BBC news (never UTV's news unless it was on at a different time to BBC's). He knew he would have an agonising further five minutes as *The Magic Roundabout* was on before the news starting at twenty to six.

For a few minutes, speaking was permitted, but it was only Ma and Da's voices that made use of the consent; my older siblings let them do the talking. Irene and Val who also went to the grammar school and had the same treacherous journey home on late school finishes, knew only too well the possible trappings of getting back across Craigavon Bridge to the relative security of the Waterside. So they either had to voice the reality of Hazel's situation that would worry Ma even more, or say nothing — lying wasn't an option. We were all so accustomed to sectarian events, as was the whole population of Northern Ireland, that no one dared pretend to be optimistic or be assumptive. Everyone would just wait for reality to be confirmed and avoided such bland wasteful words as "Hazel'll be all right" or "don't worry, she'll be home any minute now". I guessed that Da was focusing on the bombings and the damage they might have caused whilst he watched the second hand go round on the mantelpiece carriage clock. Simultaneously, Ma was focusing on Hazel and her safety whilst putting the plates of fried food and two full pots of steaming tea on the table. Their words were

171

lost in two monologues taking shape at the same time on the same stage. The words of Dougal, Florence, Dylan and Zebedee from *The Magic Roundabout* were also lost; Da had turned down the sound. I was left trying to make sense of their shaking and nodding heads, waving arms and jerky movements as they moved around the grey-black screen. It was impossible to create a narrative without hearing their voices, but I could guess that Dougal and Dylan were guilty of some misdemeanour, Florence had come to their rescue and Zebedee issued a message of morals and ethics in his best preacher-soft voice. This is how narratives played out each day, though the scenes never significantly changed. Another repetitive scene was being played out in our house, and another across the Foyle over the town. It never ceases to amaze me over the years how we can all play out repetitive scenes of one form or another, yet fail to recognise at any point that we are doing this without any renewed perspective to alter the script. Therefore, the scene, the characters (us too, of course), the relationships between the characters, their actions or their dialogue rarely changes. It often takes some external force, often by the introduction of a new character who has not been involved in such narratives, to bring about change — or at least challenge the status quo of the present scene. Unfortunately, with regard to the Troubles, any person who tried to bring about a new perspective, whether it was a president of the United States, the British prime minister or the leaders of countries that weren't seen as the West, such as Libya or Iran, would be labelled as biased by one side of the religious divide or by the other. So, further arguments and further finger-pointing would ensue, followed by the continuation of hard-line stances and the continuation of the status quo. Not surprisingly, the Troubles went on for as long as it did. Less surprisingly too, is the fatalistic evidence that hard-line stances still exist in the now more peaceful province.

It was now twenty minutes to six, so Da turned the big round knob on the side of the telly clockwise and the volume was restored just in time to hear the jingle that announced the start of the BBC Northern Ireland's news programme. Eating tea was temporarily suspended; the unwritten rule of doing absolutely nothing when the jingle came on was adhered to by everyone. When knives and forks would eventually resume their duty of feeding our mouths, they would do so in absolute reverence. They would touch the clay plate with extreme sensitivity so to not make the disturbing and irritating sound of steel on china. Not that the sound itself would prevent the hearing of the newsreader, or the reporter's interviews or the views of innocent bystanders at a bombed-out scene created by terrorists, but that Da would not tolerate a sound of any kind in case he missed a single word spoken. It was always easier for all of us, excluding Da, to maintain fasting for a short while, but when we knew that the glorious heat of the glorious fried food was losing its temperature and edibility, fasting became much more difficult. I was the first to attempt to start eating again, but only after the main headlines and updates on the car bombs that had gone off over the Derry side had been announced. It was a risk of sorts to stick my fork into the fried mince, but to attempt this manoeuvre too soon pushed up the risk stakes considerably. It also raised the level of physical punishment that Da would dish out (at least to me or Paul) or, at the very least, increase the decibels of his guttural roar in chastisement that could have been directed at any of us, except Ma — he was wise to his limits.

Death data was the main source of news that Da sought. Once the figures or estimated figures of fatalities or of the injured had been announced, Da would ease off his gatekeeper's role and allow some movement necessary for eating. Some decorum would still have to be adhered to, however.

Just as a latecomer to any church service who had to manoeuvre an old iron latch and break the monasterial silence within, so too did the rattling of the glass vestibule door into the hallway break our monastic eating. All heads turned and all bodies froze as Hazel opened the kitchen door looking windswept and rain-battered.

"The bloody bombs meant we had to walk all the way from the bridge," she screamed. 'Bloody' was seen as swearing in our house, but neither Ma nor Da checked her on this occasion.

174

"Gosh, that's a relief, you're home. We were beginning to get worried," Ma blurted. I knew Ma well enough that her insides were turning inside out, but as usual she filtered her concern. Unfortunately, for us, it almost seemed as if she wasn't that concerned or cared that much, but deep down we knew this. Hazel knew this too, so Ma's stoical response to bombs going off and her grave worry didn't rub off on her or prevent her from telling her story in true passionate style. Hazel always wore her emotions on her sleeve as it were, just as the Spanish would in *El Cid* or *For Whom the Bell Tolls*. There was always an animation of expression about this passion, which would seem at times to me as bordering on the insane, or at the very least, as conveying anger or impatience. However, this same passion would bring to life a film on the Spanish Civil War when the communists, the guerrilla fighter, with his high energy and underdog spirit would attempt to bring down the fascists played by genteel and boring characters. Hazel had this spirit in her blood and could easily have played a senorita who ran a Spanish inn full of drunken pirates after they pillaged one of Her Majesty's ships as it made its way to the Cape of Good Hope. She would boss the drunken rogues with her fiery red hair and fiery red temper, with a presence and voice that would reduce the most macho of them to passive compliance. It was so incredibly ironic, and indeed fitting, that she would later study Spanish at university, meet a Spaniard on her year out, return after her degree, marry this man, have his babies and never permanently return to the walls of Derry.

The emotion-fuelled Hazel continued.

"We got on the bus from school after our hockey match in the wind and rain, and got off at the depot on Foyle Street. We had the usual dirty looks from gangs of Catholics who spotted our blazers and were on their way home too. Just normal stuff, but I was glad I had my hockey stick with me just in case. Then we got to the top deck of Craigavon Bridge and the bus just stopped. We looked out of the window and could see an army checkpoint was being set up and the RUC were stopping traffic from moving. Within minutes, it was full of cars, vans, lorries and buses. We hadn't seen anything or heard anything so guessed there had been a warning of a bomb or something. Then we heard that there had been a warning of car bombs in Foyle Street — we'd just come from there! Everyone started screaming on the bus even though we were away from Foyle Street now. I screamed too out of sheer relief and shock. There was no point staying on the bus; it was going nowhere. We knew the army would be checking all vehicles and drivers' licences as they always did. So we were allowed to get off after the RUC checked each of us on the bus in case we were the IRA. As if they would be so stupid to plant bombs and then jump on a bus knowing full well that checkpoints would pop up all over the place. We got off the bus on the bridge and walked straight into the sleet and wind, and the dark.

We got halfway across and then we heard them go off — three of them. They were deafening, being so close. We couldn't see anything because of the buildings but it wasn't long before we could smell the smoke and hear the sirens and helicopters."

Hazel's voice now began to quiver a bit. No one interrupted her. She didn't move from her standing position in front of the sideboard. Da hadn't turned down the telly so Hazel was competing against the BBC's Gloria Hunniford, so that just increased the volume of Hazel's narrative. Having to shout above nine others in a house our size was good training for a career such as teaching or football management; Gloria was no match.

"Me, Barbara and Susan started screaming along with lots of others walking or in their cars. Nobody knew what might happen next. It wouldn't be the first time there'd be shots fired at the soldiers or RUC on the bridge or the first time there'd be more bombs going off on the Waterside where we were headed. We started running. It wouldn't take us long to get down Duke Street and up Bond's Hill, and then home. We were so frightened; it didn't matter that we'd just played hockey for an hour, we just ran. By the time we got to the railway station, we could see across the Foyle and could see the flames and smoke from Foyle Street. We could see blue flashing lights everywhere and hear the sirens. There were two helicopters out as well. We had to walk up Bond's Hill; we just couldn't run any further. My legs were aching and my shoulders were sore from carrying the two bags. We got to Susan's house in York Street first and then me and Barbara split up round the corner. It didn't matter that it was pitch black after we split because there were loads of people out anyway — the sleet didn't put them off having a good gawk across the town. The Carlins and the Browns and the Hegartys were out as usual. I was surprised you weren't out, Da."

"He was out but came in to hear the news," I blurted. I didn't dare look at him as I knew I'd see a glare from his piercing, dark brown eyes.

It wasn't long before a sense of normality emerged in the house: Ma asked about having something to eat, Hazel said she needed a bath, eating tea resumed and the rest of the evening Da intermittently disappeared into the front room with the wireless to get half hour news bulletins — that he duly repeated to us all on his return to the kitchen. The bombings and the sirens during the Troubles tragically became normality in the province. Fear was forever present in lives — the severity of it just moved up and down the scale, depending on events that happened all around us, on the telly, on people's lips. Of course, there was still the usual growing up incidents involving street gangs, bullies, child molesters, delinquents, abusive teachers, abusive parents, street dogs, the dark lanes and the subsequent nightmares, to rack up the fear.

It was the combination of a dark night and a stalker that set the scene of the other main incident that

178

involved Hazel. This time the drama took place on a non-school day, a dark Sabbath.

Living at the bottom of Alfred Street brought unusual darkness, even on the lightest of summer nights. The road that ran along the bottom of the four streets, and that acted as a tightly knit hem to join them together, had no street lights along it. The lights that did exist on the streets were no brighter than the old Victorian gas variety, were sparsely dotted along each street and would take ages to be fixed by the Department of the Environment if they were on the blink. So venturing out alone was always a scary experience, even before teatime on a winter's evening. I would test out me sprinting prowess if I were out on the street on me own; a ten-second sprint would take me away from the bottom road, up beyond the brow of the hill and to where I could hear traffic and see the bigger lights of Dale's Chemist on the corner of Glendermott Road and Limavady Road. I would still have to navigate the dark lane that ran across the top of each street. It acted as the top hem of the Four Streets and from which dark lanes ran down at right angles behind the terraced houses like perfect seams. I'd walk from a few houses beyond the brow of the hill to this junction with the top lane, and then have a six-yard burst to take me past it. Sometimes I'd muster enough courage to glance to my right and look briefly at the dark lane. If I thought I saw some shadowy figure or figures in the depths of the darkness, I'd sprint all the way to the lights and noise of Limavady

Road, so the short burst would be twenty yards instead of six. It was like getting from third base to make a home run — relief, excitement and achievement were plentiful, only there wasn't a crowd or a team mate to share the moment with. A sense of self-fulfilment was enough for me; as long as I knew I'd achieved a goal or conquered adversity, that was enough for me. I didn't need any endorsement or heaped praise from any other quarter, and therefore my inner confidence grew from an inner satisfaction. I'm not surprised it took me decades to accept praise and compliments from others and acknowledge how external endorsement of an achievement can be very powerful and give that inner confidence an immeasurable supercharged boost. However, at a young age, I didn't seek praise from others and didn't have a desire to boast about sprinting up the street in superfast time, or brag about many goals I'd scored in the last kick-about, or how many girls I'd kissed in the playground. I'm not surprised I tend to dislike those who do boast or brag or seek praise from others. Such people were labelled 'bummers' in Derry. They would 'bum themselves up', as Ma would often comment with a disdainful look, and make out they were bigger in status than they were in reality. Not surprisingly, I eventually stopped using that term after crossing the Irish Sea; connotations were both endless and disturbingly inappropriate beyond the intended Derry meaning.

The last street light on at the bottom of each of the

Four Streets was usually positioned outside the third last house from the bottom. So, if Da went out to the garage round the corner on the bottom road, he would always take his red box torch as it was pretty dark. No one but Da would go out to the garage to get anything on their own. On any rare occasion that someone wanted to go in there after darkness fell, it was never without Da; even then it was scary. Saying that, nothing was stored there except anything to do with Da — mainly bits of wood, partially filled bags of cement or sand, a shovel for when the snow came, odd building bricks, a vice and stuff to do with repairing the rust on a car and car cleaning and polishing stuff. The garage was really to keep the car safe from car thieves, though car crime wasn't something that was really prevalent in the Four Streets or even in the local area. Da was ultra-hot on security, so the garage was built and secured by a huge padlock. Da's treasured tools and anything of value was kept in the shed in the backyard.

Me and Paul had gone to bed about nine o'clock as usual, and as usual after a glass of milk and a digestive biscuit before kneeling on a vinyl-coloured chair in the kitchen and our saying of the Lord's Prayer. It always felt awkward and embarrassing doing this in front of everyone else. Da insisted this rule, though we were convinced it never applied to any of our siblings, and we never saw our younger sister of six years have to go through such a humiliating ritual. We were convinced that Da felt he was doing something for his bit for a

Christian ethos that was embedded in our designated church, All Saints Clooney, but that we knew only too well was riddled with hypocrisy and bigotry. In fact, it's fair to say, that most people in our locality thought the same, and me ma too, but refused to publicly say it for fear of being ostracised and labelled as a heathen.

So we had gone to bed, me in the darkness of the lower bunk and Paul in the semi-lightness of the top bunk. It was a cold night so once we left the warmth of the kitchen fire, it was a sprint up the stairs and into bed. We weren't allowed to say a word in case we woke up baby sister Isobel who had been put in her cot an hour or so before, so any sprinting was done on tiptoes. The chimney breast separated our bunk beds from her cot and created such a limited view that when me head was on the pillow, I couldn't even see the cot sides. It was a Saturday night so Da had made the beds for us and not Ma. It was always a hard job squeezing into the tightly packed sheet and blankets that Da had pressed under the mattress. He had never been in the army but I'm sure he would easily had won the best bed-maker award. Once I buried meself under the bedclothes and me breath had warmed the bed with the help of the hot water bottle that Ma had placed half an hour before, I closed me eyes tight so as not to imagine scary figures wondering around the dimly lit depressing bedroom. I obviously fell asleep and didn't hear Ma and Da come to bed, though that was the norm.

The next thing I heard was the shrieks of Hazel as

she burst into the bedroom, shouting, "Da, Da, wake up, there's a man after me!" I could make out Hazel's torso through the small 'window' between the top of my bed and the bottom of Paul's, bordered by the wooden uprights, my bed and the spring bottom of the upper bunk. She stood in the small space between our bunk beds and the door, blocking out most of the tiny radiance coming from the landing light. Da was out of bed like a shot; he was always a light sleeper despite the tiredness that came from the exhausting schedule at work followed by a slightly less exhausting schedule at home. He had his blue, red and white striped pyjamas on. His face was pale and, what was left of his hair, was hanging just like Bobby Charlton's, dry without Brylcreem and flopping the wrong way on his head. In a flash, he'd grabbed the black torch he kept under the bed for when he had to pee in the pot during the night, threw on his maroon dressing gown and stepped into his tartan slippers and then off out of the bedroom door. The urgency of the situation was clearly reflected by the fact he didn't tie his dressing gown.

Nothing else was spoken in the room till after Da had gone. Then Ma asked Hazel what had happened and was she okay. Hazel had put the light on and had plonked herself on Ma and Da's bed by now, and was sobbing uncontrollably. At some point she had reassured Ma that she was all right and then told her story of what had happened, though there were many interrupted and unfinished sentences during the retelling. Hazel's storytelling always contained a sense of high drama, even if the story was merely a recollection of how me and Paul had refused to obey her orders to come in when she'd been instructed by Ma to go out and fetch us in for bedtime. She would add a bit of spice and sensationalism to our stubbornness by adding something to what and how we had replied to her and end up getting a bigger scolding as a consequence! So, the retelling of her story of having someone following her in the dark was like that of the biggest Mexican bandit's wife who had been captured by sheriff Gregory Peck, and then returned to him to pass on orders to surrender. Her account would be spiced up by adding how she'd been tortured and humiliated by Peck and his crew and that her husband's masculinity depended on how he was going to defend her honour. A bit of spice adds bite to all dishes!

Hazel had gone to Bible meeting earlier in the evening at Ebrington Presbyterian Church hall with her friends Janet and Barbara. Val had usually gone with her too but had a cold virus so had given it a miss. I'd heard previous heated conversations about this meeting as Da wasn't happy for them to go to a Presbyterian church function as he saw Presbyterians as heathens, not like the so-called 'proper' Christians who belonged to his Church of Ireland brethren. He also saw these folk, as being one step away from the Free Presbyterians who, according to him, belonged to a church that was founded by none other than the Reverend Ian Paisley, a man he saw as creating his own interpretation of the Bible and therefore creating a whole new set of beliefs. The fact that Paisley talked in the same way that he preached, with shouting, much ferocity and hatred of all things Catholic, added to his scepticism of such a Christian ethos.

Hazel and Val had argued that they were going to a Christian gathering and that all Protestants and Catholics were Christian regardless of the name of a church or the name given to someone who belonged to it. They argued too that the meeting was about singing songs about Jesus, praying to God, organised by a clergyman and was therefore a highly respectable place. I'm not sure what Da had thought of their argument that would not have been out of place at their school's debating society events, but I was convinced this was all a sham. I knew they weren't interested by any form of Christian worship, and like me and all me siblings, were forced to attend Sunday school, Bible class and church services on Sundays because of Da's (and Ma's to a lesser extent) sense of shame if the family didn't buy into 'belonging' to the Church. 'Belonging' really meant being actively involved, being seen in the church hall, being seen in the church, being a brownie or a cub scout (including doing 'Bob a Job'!) and going on the annual Sunday school summer excursion to Portrush. So I couldn't understand why they would want to attend a church-based event that wasn't being forced upon them. Then one day I'd overheard Hazel and Val talking about this Bible meeting and about which boys would be there and which ones they fancied. I overheard many conversations as it seemed to me that neither me nor Paul really existed in their eyes and were totally pre-occupied by all things football. Although they were right about our obsession about the big round ball, it didn't mean we were also deaf. We both felt that our big sisters just didn't think we were cognisant of their conversations. It was almost as if we were regularly sprinkled by Merlin's dust to become invisible, even though we were actually in the same room as them.

To be honest, I didn't blame them for lying to Da. Our house on a Sunday was quiet and we weren't allowed out unless to church or a quick trip to the sweet shop. Early Sunday evening viewing on the telly was boring as it had the News, *Songs of Praise* or some documentary about a public figure in Northern Ireland who, because of their good Christian work, had warranted a programme being filmed about them. It never ceased to amuse me that although Da was bound to have had his suspicions about me sisters' religious excursions on a Sunday evening, or indeed, suspicions about anything, he never voiced them in an argument. He was a man whose views were founded on evidence and proof. If he didn't have this, and we were all good at avoiding giving him any of this, his views would be purely circumstantial and assumptive — and he'd look both weak and a fool. He knew too that Ma would vehemently oppose him if he had no clear evidence.

Hazel continued her account that she and her friends had gone to the meeting at the church hall, they'd all taken their time leaving and had spent some time chatting outside after the hall had been locked up. I pictured them having a good laugh with boys but couldn't bring meself to imagine any kissing between them and boys — that was just not possible in me head. Nevertheless, although Hazel didn't necessarily lie about who was there with her, she didn't say anything about boys being present. She said that 'they' had all lost track of time and as it had got a bit late, she and Janet thought it best to walk Barbara back to the bottom of Chapel Road as she'd become frightened to walk the fifteen minutes there on her own. On the walk back, she and Janet became aware of a man walking about fifty yards behind them as they walked along Clooney Terrace. They kept a close eye on him and had speeded up a bit. By the time Hazel said goodbye to Janet on the edge of the Four Streets, she saw the man go towards York Street, two streets away from Alfred Street. Hazel said she "ran like the clappers" down Alfred Street just to make sure she got home safely. Like all of us, we didn't like being at the foot of the street and could only see darkness beyond the bottom of the street, reaching past the Tins, the railway line and the river. The bright lights on the city side were of no comfort as they seemed miles away.

Hazel went on to say that she had to stop outside the front door and try and find her house key in her bag.

Normally she would have got it out of her bag as she'd walk down the street and have it ready to go into the small hole in the door lock. As she'd been running, she wasn't prepared. She said that she was panicking so much that she couldn't find the key. Then as she finally found it and put it into the hole, the man appeared from round the corner out of the blackness. She screamed like a banshee and rushed into the house and up the stairs to get Da. I wouldn't have been surprised if Da had heard the key turn in the lock with the one ear he kept open, never mind the scream!

Ma didn't interrupt her talking and didn't ask her any questions; she was good at doing that. I could feel my own heart beating faster as Hazel sobbed and staggered her way through her story. Although I could at last breathe properly when her story came to a close, I was also disappointed with the anti-climax of it all: if the man had followed her into the house and she'd continued screaming; if she'd run over to the fireplace and then hit him over the head with the iron poker and his skull had given in to the force. If, if, if, if only — the ending would have reflected the main story. Instead, there was an abrupt ending to her story and a drop in the drama in the room.

Paul had joined me from his top bunk and was now on the edge of me bed, but as the adrenalin shrank in our bodies the opposite happened in our body temperatures. Our feet on the lino felt the coldness first so we jumped under the bedclothes of me bed — extraordinary events always warranted unusual reactions and behaviours. Before long the dull-lit bedroom housed everyone else in the house, even Robin, who wasn't easily roused from his slumber. Ma re-enacted Hazel's story but with calmer, less breathlessness and subtle changes in order to give a more measured and less emotive version of her account. She knew only too well that Irene and Val and baby sister Isobel would be freaked out by her retelling, never mind what Hazel's retelling would have triggered in them. Mina and Robin had such a laid-back attitude to anything that Hazel's own account wouldn't have fazed them.

It wasn't long before we heard the hall door close and Da making his way back up the stairs. Normally he would have hated such a gathering in his bedroom; he hated fuss and couldn't cope with the collective fuss and collective stress that his offspring could muster in circumstances like this. He would normally have loudly shouted at everyone's presence in his bedroom, that we were all being ridiculous, and send everyone packing back to their own night-time places of slumber. This time, and in such similar times of having a captivated audience, he made the most of giving us an update. It was a bit like the bedroom scene from *Mary Poppins* when the children all gathered on the bed, but instead of Mary Poppins talking and singing, it was Minnie on the bed with the children (me sisters with their nylon dressing gowns on) and only Bertie doing the talking. In order to see Da properly, me and Paul moved to the top bunk whilst Robin sat on the edge of me bed. There was no singing.

Da spoke of how he ran with his torch round the corner of the house, round the back of the garage and then up the lane that ran at the back of our house. He then proceeded to run down the next lane and up the next one till he'd check out all the five lanes that bordered and separated the Four Streets. He had decided that the man would have wanted to hide somewhere in the dark of night and that no one would have dared search for him. Not only were the lanes uneven with part gravel, part concrete, part tarmac, part mud and part grass, there were also many lumps of dog mess made by the numerous dogs in the neighbourhood that were let out by their owners during the day — either for hours or just to do their business. Da had thought of the Tins being a good place for the man to take refuge, but decided against that as the lights from over the town would have given a smattering of light across this wasteland. The silhouette of the man would have been easier to spot if he had been moving around. Da also ruled out this option as the Tins would have trapped the man to a degree, whereas getting up to the top of the Four Streets would have given him the freedom of reaching numerous places, including his home.

Eventually he had given up the chase and came home, though not before bumping into a drunken Eric Molloy from across the street, who had stumbled home from a drinking session at his friend Bobby Henderson's house in Bond Street. The pubs, of course, were not open on Sundays in Derry at that time, courtesy of the God-fearing Protestants who preached that there was no place for alcohol, drunkenness and any so-called heathen-induced activities on the Sabbath. Da, of course, never turned down an invitation to have a chat, and once Eric had said the magic words of "Hello, Bertie", that was it; Da was in a conversation and the retelling of the recent events. Eric had said he hadn't seen anyone, though was also quick to point out that the 'wee whiskey' he'd had before leaving Bobby's had blurred his vision somewhat.

There was suddenly nothing else to be said about the whole event so Da ordered everyone to go back to bed. Me sisters all looked frozen by now anyway and didn't hang about to challenge Da's command. I knew that Da was dying to question Hazel about her being out late in the first place and getting herself into this situation in the first place, but he didn't. I knew too, that he knew that Ma would have been furious with him if he had dared to make Hazel's situation worse by telling her off, or at the very least, challenge her. I knew that he would only leave that till teatime the next day — he would have had to get it out of his system first and therefore wait till the shock and strong emotion of it all had settled down. He knew too, that Ma was less likely to stop him the next day.

By the time Da had switched off the light, me head was whirling with imaginings of what had happened.

There was no way I was going to get back to sleep for ages. I created pictures in me head of the man. He wore a wet, dark, baggy suit, a dirty white shirt without a tie, black steel-capped boots and a dark cloth cap that showed a long black-haired fringe draping down his forehead. His nose was chiselled to a perfect point and was nestled amongst high cheek bones that made his lower face sink in as it met a square chin that had owned a new, moon-shaped, thin scar — a la *Peaky Blinders*. His eyes were deeply sunk into their sockets and were drowned by overarching black bushy eyebrows. He walked with a limp that became more pronounced when he ran. I pictured him dragging his left leg that had previously been crushed by the rear wheels of a farmer's tractor when he failed to get out of his way when poaching for rabbits. The dark lane of which he ran up, would have been a real struggle, but pure fear got him to the top of the Four Streets and on his way to the safety of his hovel home off Chapel Road.

When I was woken up the next morning for school by Ma, I didn't know what I had imagined and what had actually happened the night before. Everything had just seemed a nightmare when I thought about it over me cornflakes. What was definitely real, was Hazel saying to Ma over her toast and tea, she would never stay out late again. Ma knew that this declaration would be a temporary one, but heard what she needed to hear for now. We all make declarations to changes of behaviour or attitude after an episode of ill-judgement and the subsequent fallout of this. We can feel morally stronger and a better person for such declarations, and as long as we can carry out our 'promises' for a decent length of time, we're not too bothered or self-critical when we eventually lapse as is our fallible way.

# Chapter 10
# Val, the Fourth-born Daughter

Val. She was only three years older than me and therefore had much more contact with me in me early years. She flitted between doing big sister stuff with Hazel and doing more kiddie stuff with me and Paul. She was definitely one of me four older sisters who didn't judge or mock or criticise or bully to the same degree as the other three — I was definitely closer to her. Age can be such a factor in sibling relationships. You can feel part of someone's life, have more in common and feel an affection for a sibling when the age gap is two or three, but greater than that, the roles have much less of an equity about them. An older sibling can feel so detached from you that they're almost from a second family but at the same time related to you. Having a much older sibling can sometimes feel like having another parent or parents. There's no doubt that there can be a degree of positive nurturing that can be experienced, and I'm sure that this took place for me — but it wasn't constant enough for me to feel it or remember it. As is typical of us as we reflect on our childhoods, negative memories can block out the positive ones, unless the positive ones far outweigh the other. So for me, Val unknowingly changed this rigid and imprinted pattern.

I don't think I was any different to any other child in looking for affection and a close bond with another. I also definitely don't fit into the category of many children around the world who are deprived of many things in their own worlds and where deprivation *is* their existence. Affection would be far down their priority list of needs when the basics of food, shelter and clothing are substantially lacking.

Don't get me wrong, there were numerous times when I felt really connected to the 'bigger' Kennedy family, but these were short-lived affairs. Looking at other big families in the Four Streets I'd sense there was a togetherness that we didn't have, but then again, they probably thought the same of the Kennedys. Viewing a family structure from the outside is not the same as living, experiencing and feeling it from the inside. The obvious 'Public versus Private' world of families (and of individuals, of course) springs to mind! I'd often reflect on this 'dysfunction' within our undoubted functional family and try to figure out what went wrong in our family relationships and what happened to me feeling disconnected. I have often wondered what impact staying in hospital with me bruised shoulder after I was born might have had on me; when Ma and me twin brother had gone home without me. Did that leave me with a sense of disconnectedness? Leave me with attachment issues? I don't think so. Connectedness to others has got to be nurtured, got to be earned, got to be developed — and takes effort. It's not something that is, *just is*. I get the whole 'blood is thicker than water' thing; there's something natural about a family connection that is unexplainable, but it is a psychological thing, not something based on feeling and experiencing. Take, for example, someone adopted — they can have a feeling of a sense of connection with their adopted parents but once they become aware of their natural parents, connections to these new people in their lives can emerge as this new information affects their psychological state and ultimately influences their feeling state.

Of course, none of this theorising went on in me head to allow me and Val to be closer; everything was about whether or not I enjoyed spending time with her. Saying that, I don't remember a single time when I played games or spent time with Val on me own. Any time would have been shared with at least one other, most often, Paul. There were many other boys who wanted to share Val's affections and attention besides me and Paul. As Val was a mere three years older than me, many of the boys in the Four Streets who I hung out with were roughly the same age as me, but the boys who I looked to gain some crumbs of street credit from were a couple or more years older than me. As a ten-year-old boy I was totally oblivious to sex, sexual relationships and romance. As far as I was concerned, girls ruined what boys (or men) did. I'd seen too many heroic and brave cowboys, sheriffs, knights, generals and heroes such as Robin Hood and Zorro fall from heroic grace because of a weakness in being attracted to, or manipulated by a romantic liaison with, a woman or girl. Not only did they portray a flaw in their masculine strength, their love or affection for a woman would interfere with a well-planned operation, a cunning plot, a daring raid, an act of bravery or the just killing of an evil villain. We all know what happened to Samson! So, when the older boys started to ask questions about Val or eye her from head to toe or wolf-whistle at her, a whole new perspective of her and girls in general opened up for me.

I was only ten, but still in primary school. I was yet to experience what heralded for the likes of me at the big school, but seeing how me sisters and older boys in the Four Streets changed once they left the bosom of primary and suckled the fruits of secondary's Eden, I had an inkling. I was innocently oblivious to puberty and how the bodies of me sisters changed during their teenage years — they were just me sisters. Boobs were just parts of their bodies, nothing to be attracted to or be lusted over or be viewed in some kind of sexual manner. I had a lot to learn.

The portrayal of romance and physical and sexual attraction in films and television dramas in the early seventies were nothing compared to what we'd get accustomed to being portrayed decades later. The dancers from *Top of the Pops*, Pans People, were pretty mild in sexual symbolism compared to the pelvic writhing and thrusting that Madonna, Beyoncè and Britney Spears would bring to Thursday nights on BBC1 over the next few decades. So too, the gentle kissing between Gene Kelly and Rita Hayworth (when lips never moved in a kiss and stuck like superglue for a few seconds) was me sex education as a young lad. This was in mighty contrast to the passionate snogging and 'eating the other's face' prior to full-blown sex that became the norm across our cinema and TV screens. As a ten-year-old, I never imagined any romantic encounter going beyond kissing, just as I never looked to investigate where babies came from. I guess, just as the two-dimensional lives on the telly had no depth or substance, so too was me view of life around me, devoid of hidden substance, meaning or adult depth.

So, when the likes of Wee John Wark or Marty Murphy or Gavin Paine asked me questions about Val's underwear and if I'd seen her knickers or bra or naked body, I was totally embarrassed. Me face would glow like the red-hot lava of a volcano — not because I *knew* that these were sexually orientated questions, but because I knew that there was something rude and 'not right' about them. Me face would red up so quickly and I would become frozen in the intensity of full body heat, that I couldn't even try to fake answers to gain some street credit points. I couldn't even make up stories about seeing me sister in the bath or walking around her bedroom in just bra and knickers. When they would tease me that I had sneaky peeks at me sisters through keyholes, I'd just die on the spot. It was years and years before I could handle such embarrassing moments — especially if it related to anything sexual. In fact, it was years before I knew what 'anything sexual' meant!

I remember one embarrassing situation in particular when I was hanging about with Marty Murphy's younger brother Sean (who was a year younger than me). Well, it started as one embarrassing moment, but then turned into two. There wasn't any game going on and Paul had stayed indoors as he occasionally did, whereas I was outside as usual. So, Sean suggested we go to the backyard of his house on King Street. I hadn't been there before and I knew that Ma and Da would clearly give me a telling-off if they knew I was going there. They had their own snobbish 'Protestant' ways when it came to social status. A family who they saw as poor or bone idle, and on the dole, or constantly looked unkempt or dirty in their eyes, which reflected a family with lower values and norms to their own, was a family they didn't want any of us to have anything to do with. Ma and Da knew that there were many families who lived in the Four Streets and who fitted this type (religion wasn't a defining or relevant factor), so they knew that me and Paul would be playing with boys from these families, but they didn't want us to build close bonds with them. Hanging around their houses was a definite no-no. It felt as if we'd catch some disease off these boys or from their families, merely by being with them. They wouldn't say such judgemental views, but instead gave focus to more realistic 'contamination' such as getting head lice or picking up swear words. They were right on both these counts. The thing is though, all the kids in the neighbourhood got lice from time to time (though I don't know why lice would be interested in me scalp to begin with as Da shaved off me hair regularly), so there was no knowing from whose scalp a louse jumped from, to get to mine. As for swearing, I wasn't much of a swearer anyway. I thought it was wrong in some way — but there was no way I'd actually swear in front of Ma or Da; fear of the penalty of such a sin saw to that. So there was no way of Ma or Da knowing if I contracted any swear disease from the likes of the Murphys, the Magilloways, the Burns or anyone for that matter.

I knew that going to the Murphy's backyard with Sean wasn't a good idea for a number of reasons. Sean was always keen to win the approval from his bigger brothers and from any of the older boys. He always wanted to look big and macho in their eyes and therefore would do stupid things just to try and impress them. He'd smoke a cigarette, swear a lot, have a few mouthfuls of beer or have a fight with anyone of their choosing if he thought he'd 'fit in' and be seen as 'big'. Stupid actions often had stupid consequences so that was one reason to be worried about going with him. Boredom sure feeds stupid actions! The Murphy's backyard was always filthy, stank of dogs and had all kinds of rubbish dumped there — so that was another risk factor.

The less rational reason for not going with Sean was because of the house's location. The houses in King Street backed on to a wider lane than those of the others in the Four Streets which was dwarfed by the twenty-foot wall of the navy (army) base, Ebrington Barracks. There were even higher lookout posts, just like Colditz, that cornered the barracks. I feared both the army and the RUC and the thought of getting on the wrong side of the law. So, when walking up the King Street lane I always felt I was being watched by the army, their camera lenses would zoom in on me, they'd do their security checks to see if I was a terrorist or to find some reason to arrest me. I had nothing to be arrested for, but then again, I'd heard countless stories from others, of people being arrested for doing nothing wrong. So when me and Sean walked up the lane and scaled the six-foot backyard wall, avoiding the pieces of broken glass cemented into the top of it, I tried to look as nonchalant and as innocent as possible. Any hope of not drawing attention to us from the lookout posts was blown away when Sean stood on the wall and gave two fingers to any camera or squaddie that was looking at us.

Jumping down into the yard was made easy as an old discarded mattress was beneath us, but the mixture of brown and yellow stains didn't invite a welcome. I'd have to make sure I landed on me feet and not end up putting me hands on the stains, or worse still, doing a roly-poly and having me whole body touch them; I couldn't even tell if they were still wet! Feeling more and more nervous by the second left me feeling very vulnerable to an attack of embarrassment. The older boys were definitely due to tease me at some point, so I jumped. The springs had gone completely in the centre so me planned two-footed landing went pear-shaped. Me left foot sunk deeper into the mattress than me right so I fell to one side and landed on me back. The roar of laughter echoed round the brick-bordered yard and me face went red. Me face slowly went back to its normal pale colour and I thought that was it as far as going red was concerned — how wrong I was. I could never totally relax in the company of these big boys anyway, and I could feel me body tense from head to toe. The traditional pecking order would inadvertently lead to the hierarchy picking on the subordinates, either physically, mentally or emotionally, or a combination of them. The next instalment of embarrassment really took me by surprise and left me burning red, but also totally and utterly confused.

I'd thought I had passed through one rite of passage by having a long drag on an Embassy cigarette as proof of me 'manliness', but unlike Sean who puffed and puffed like a pro, I coughed and coughed till tears ran down me face. The big boys' laughter didn't bring out the burning red in me as I'd at least had one inhalation and I therefore didn't feel an absolute waster — but then came the magazine. I'd often heard the reference to 'dirty magazines' but had no idea what they were about. All I knew was that they were something secret and within the realms of 'the forbidden'. They were also magazines that only boys could look at so I knew they had something to do with girls. In me innocence I thought they might be a bit like the women's underwear pages in the Marshall Ward catalogue that Ma got. I'd look at these out of curiosity but I guess something more subliminally sexual was at the root of this secret viewing, even though I was too young to have any physical or emotional response as a result of these peeking sessions. However, the dirty magazine that was thrust into me hand by Sean's brother Micky was definitely nothing like the Marshall Ward catalogue. He commanded me to look at every single page or I wouldn't be allowed to leave the backyard. I'm not sure how many pages I turned over as fast as I could, but I didn't reach the end. The pictures of women's naked boobs were not too much of a shock. I'd never seen me sisters' boobs naked enough to show their nipples but was aware of the general shape and size of them. The temperature of the burning in me face rose quite a few degrees when I saw the pubic hairs between their legs, but when I turned a page that displayed a naked woman lying on her back with her legs fully spread to reveal the hidden depths beneath the pubic hairs, the temperature shot up. Me face burned and burned. Me embarrassment was as the big boys had probably predicted, but when Micky shouted, "That's where your willy goes, and I'd put mine in your sister any day," me burning was molten metal hot, just like Da's blowtorch when heating his soldering iron. Me head spun around with confusion as well as embarrassment. I couldn't fathom the idea of me willy inside a girl. How would I do that? Why would I do that? What would happen if I did? I was lost in utter 'blindness'. I just thought all of this was rude and wrong. As for Micky's willy being in me sister, me mind went blank and me body froze. Was Val's and me other sisters' bodies like this? Fear took hold of me, not because I was under threat, but to indicate that I had to get away as fast as possible before I would pass out! I had just about enough awareness to see that the older boys were in fits of laughter — now was my chance. So I instinctively sprang to me feet, climbed the side wall like a monkey and legged it over the wall. The pain of catching me knee on the cemented glass at the top of the back wall didn't deter me.

I could still hear the boys' laughter amidst their swearing that I'd escaped, as I ran down the lane. I managed a quick glance behind me to make sure I wasn't being chased — I wasn't. Their eyes were no longer on me but as I glanced, I caught sight of the army post and was sure the security cameras were on me. There were no bombings to alert them or IRA men climbing the high wall to distract them, so they must have been looking at me out of boredom, if nothing else. The soldiers would have had no idea of why I was running like the wind, I knew that. The mind, though, can play tricks on us in such panic situations. So me distorted thinking led me to believe that they too knew about the embarrassment I'd just faced, how naïve and innocent I was, and how easily me face burned like the eleventh bonfire — a burning to be seen for miles around!

Once I got round the corner of the bottom of King Street I knew I was out of sight of all of the onlookers. The street was empty and the road at the bottom of the Four Streets was empty. I could stop running and take breath. As soon as I stopped, I could feel the pain of me left knee. I could now see the blood trickling slowly down me leg; I wiped it away before it hit me white socks. Da's potential anger entered me head at seeing blood-stained socks — coupled with the trauma of a barrage of interrogating questions. It was always difficult to be composed when he bombarded me with questions; they were always accusatory. I knew that if I said anything about where I was, or who I was with, or what I was doing that didn't meet his Victorian attitude of how children should behave, I'd be instantly walloped with his leather-skinned hand; the belt was only used when he'd arrive home from work and when his built-up anger from instructing his apprentices had festered. I knew he was at home. I 'prayed' that he was outside fiddling with the car or at something else in the garage. His mind would be distracted and I might only get a bit of verbals that would bolt from a contorted face. The force would send blobs of saliva into the air and leave a bit of froth on the corner of his mouth. The punishment would be swift and I could then head into the house to sort out me cut and allow me head to sort out the story that I would have to tell. I would have to edit the account to reduce further ramifications. I knew that Da would ask further questions later when he'd finish his task, but he was never at boiling point if he'd already let off some steam about the same incident earlier.

I could see that Da's car was outside the garage along the gable, but I couldn't see him. I couldn't take the risk of him not being outside so I decided to climb over the half-broken sleeper and jump into the Tins. The tall grass, the high nettles and the lofty thistles created a perfect screen from any of me friends, or anyone else for that matter. I needed time to stem the blood and to get me head straight. There were plenty of small craters in the Tins, to take refuge in, which we imagined had been created by Second World War bombs. I grabbed a handful of dock leaves to hold and press over the three-inch-long cut. Me basic first aid was learned from countless scenes of treating the wounded in the westerns and war films that I loved to watch. I knew that I had to hold the leaves firmly to stop the blood and allow it to congeal. Arriving home with a cut was one thing, but one with blood still oozing out was another! The dock leaves weren't stemming the flow. I looked around and could see an old jumper that had been dumped many months before — the Tins after all were the perfect dumping ground for waste items that people couldn't fit in their ash-tin bins. I didn't care that the jumper was dirty. As long as it did the job, it was good enough for me. Me namesake, George Kennedy, didn't worry about a bit of dirt, so I wasn't going to either. The main thing was, it worked. The blood stopped and I was able to clean any smudges of blood off me leg using a bit of me own spit. The cut was just above me knee so movement didn't aggravate it. After sitting for what seemed ages, I heard Val's voice shouting me name to come in for supper and bed. Being called in was good cover in case Da was outside. Even though I had to fight to block out the dirty magazine and Mickey's comments about Val earlier, I was still glad it was Val who got the task to fetch me in; Hazel and Irene had no patience when they would fetch me and Paul in; it was like being herded in by the Gestapo. They would rush me and tell me off if they thought I was moving too slowly, whereas Val spoke more gently and didn't make a big deal of it.

When I got in, Da wasn't around, so it was only Ma I had to explain to about me knee. I obviously made up a simple story of saying to Ma that I'd slipped and fallen on a broken bottle; there were plenty of them over the Tins. Although Ma went through her usual routine of tutting about the dangers of the Tins, she knew it was our playground, the playground for all the kids of the Four Streets. Thankfully, the cut didn't warrant stitches so Da wasn't called upon to take me to Altnagelvin hospital — he wouldn't have been happy about that. He had enough trips to A&E because of me and the others without adding another one. I was ordered to get me pyjamas on and get ready for supper. Once this order was given, I knew that that would be the end of any enquiry or interrogation or telling-off — phew! Me and Paul went to our bunk beds. Then Paul asked what really happened — he knew I was out with someone I shouldn't have been and had seen me with Sean Murphy. Normally I would have told him, but the embarrassment and confusion about the whole thing made me stay with me original story. I lay for ages going over the trauma time and time again. The dirty magazines and the naked women's bodies with their pubic hair and legs in full view didn't necessarily disturb me. The fact that me own willy, or any other boy's willy could fit inside a girl was the disturbing bit. I felt me tiny, squidgy little willy under me pyjama bottoms — it couldn't physically fit into anything I thought (I had no idea of erections). As I still couldn't fathom any proper understanding, I eventually put all of Mickey's comments down to made-up stories just to embarrass me. That was it, it was all made up. I was able to put it to rest and go to sleep. It was years later before it *did* make sense.

Thankfully, the second memory of Val was much more pleasant, though the Troubles played a more significant role in this drama. I'd heard about me sisters going to the pictures to see films that had been promoted in the *Jackie* magazine. They'd be talking about some heart-throb they'd read about and were dying to see on the big screen. They knew too though, that films seemed to take weeks before they were shipped across the Irish Sea from mainland Britain. Everyone in England, Scotland and Wales had seen the latest film weeks before us Northern Ireland folk. Even the film stars had been on Parkinson's show weeks before the reels were paddling their way across the choppy current between Britain and Ireland. Then, as if there was only one solitary reel to serve the whole population of Northern Ireland, we from Derry had to wait till everyone in Belfast had seen it and then for it to be transported by special convoy to the second biggest city, Derry.

I never really paid much attention to what might have been the topic of conversation amongst me sisters about the pictures, so was taken completely by surprise when Val announced to me and Paul that she'd take us to see *101 Dalmatians* at the Rialto. It was to be me first time. Thoughts of what it was going to be look like were based purely on what I'd seen on the telly. Huge containers of Coke and huge boxes of popcorn thrilled me brain. I'd had the rare bottle of Coke but I had no idea what popcorn tasted like. I was dying to try it out. I knew Americans did *everything* in extra-large size, but that Derry portions would be nowhere near what I imagined in me head.

Val only announced the trip on the Saturday morning of the same-day matinee, so there was not much time to get too excited. This was typical of me family; not to announce something exciting too far in advance. I guess me and Paul were pretty excitable leading up to Santa coming, Easter eggs arriving and the annual Sunday school excursion, so Ma and Da and me sisters took control of what they could, and kept 'special' announcements to the last minute. Val's revelation came shortly after me Rice Krispies (a treat) had stopped snapping, crackling and popping. *Water Boy* was about to start. It was the first Ma had heard about this trip too so we had to go through Ma's usual concerns and worries about going 'over the town' and to a building that was in the heart of the city and within its walls. The IRA tended to leave their bombs and shoot people dead within the perimeter of the walls — probably as this area symbolised Protestant heritage and the Apprentice Boys' heroics. So, Val had to reduce Ma's fears as best as possible and give bus times, film start and end times and expected home time before she was pacified. The film we were going to see was pretty irrelevant; I would have gone to see any sloppy boy-meets-girl romance — it was all about the occasion, another rite of passage!

The film was going to be shown at two fifteen p.m. so that still gave time to see *Football Focus* on BBC and *On the Ball* on ITV — or so I thought. I hadn't factored in the getting ready ceremony that Ma made me and Paul go through. We escaped a bath as that was always a Saturday night ritual, but the rest of the preparations wasn't far short of getting ready for Sunday school each

Sunday. The main difference was the clothes that we were made to wear. For the weekly trip to hear about the gospels, to read the Catechism and be preached about what a teacher's personal moral and ethical stance was, we'd be donned in a dark green suit. No, not one with trousers, one with a jacket and shorts. The shorts were duly supported by a pair of black braces. The wearing of this suit amongst me peers was yet another barrowful of embarrassment and humiliation to add to the ever-increasing heap. When was this heap ever to stop growing? When would the mocking, slagging and sarcasm stop? When would the horrible burning face extinguish before it engulfed me whole face? I guess distraction techniques to cope with this kind of catastrophe began at an early age. I'd try and zone out and give focus on something else; something in the room, in the distance, yesterday's football game, the carpet. I know that this didn't stop the burning sensation but it played a part in reducing the longevity of it. If only I'd been taught to breathe properly (mindfulness was yet to be in vogue) in such moments — the anguish would have been less intense. I'm not surprised then, that as an adult, I can easily meditate and reach a calmness through simply breathing correctly. So too, can I give such focus to a task, a moment, a thought, that I can create an impenetrable field around my being so that me status quo can remain relatively intact from whatever is trying to disturb me spirit. Me self-awareness allows me to know me fallibility and me limitations!

Thankfully, Ma didn't comprehend *the* suit for the trip to the Rialto! Beige shorts, long grey socks, brown sandals and a Fair Isle jumper that covered a navy polo shirt, was her choice. As per usual, me and Paul were dressed exactly the same except for the colour of the jumper; mine would be blue and white, whilst Paul's would be brown and white. Ma wanted to feel revolutionary and not keep to tradition and have us dressed without any distinctive differences in outfits or colour. She failed to acknowledge that I was much, much skinnier than Paul, had blonde straight hair as opposed to his thick, dark, wavy hair, and therefore we didn't even look like brothers never mind twins! The sandals were definitely Sunday best and would never get to kick a ball under any circumstances. I knew that the usual fear around keeping the sandals scuff-free would be with me but I wasn't going to let that spoil the day. Me hair didn't need washing — Da had chopped and shaved most of it the previous Saturday. However, I didn't escape the extra face and neck wash and the squeezing of the end of the face cloth into me ears to remove any dirt or bit of wax that had found residence in them. No one can ever have any idea of an individual's pain threshold when rubbing or scrubbing someone else's body, be it ears or head or genitalia. A person bases their strength and force on their own pain threshold, so when stoic Ma twisted the face cloth and then twisted it into me ear like a drill bit into a wall, she couldn't possibly know when it was time to stop before

I would jump and squeal with pain. This happened every time — definitely every school day. She would wait for me signal before stopping, but she knew if I was pretending, and push the wet piece of material in further until she got the truthful response.

All the preparations took me mind off the pending excitement that I yearned for, but it also meant that we couldn't watch Ian St John and Jimmy Greaves presenting *On the Ball*. Once it was missed, that was it, there was no recording or 'Catch up' that came to our rescue decades later, courtesy of Rupert Murdoch's empire. Once we were all ready, Ma gave Val enough money for our admission, our bus fares and sweets. I wasn't allowed to empty any of the pennies I'd saved in me red post-box piggy bank — that was to be kept for the Sunday school annual excursion to Portrush in August. So off we set up the street, holding Val's hand (Ma's orders) till we got over the brow of the hill and out of sight.

I suggested we walk and save the bus money for more sweets, but Val refused. She was responsible for us and if anything happened on foot, she'd get the blame and maybe scupper any future trips. So, we crossed the top of Bond's Hill, instead of going down it to get to Craigavon Bridge, and then waited to cross Clooney Terrace where the bus stop was. Waiting for the green man to appear (I never waited when on me own or with me mates), an army jeep suddenly pulled up virtually opposite us on the middle of the road. Six soldiers jumped out with rifles in hand. They seemed in a hurry to get out of the jeep. Val squeezed our hands tight. We froze on the spot. As each one got out, they held their rifles up to their shoulder and took aim, ready to fire if necessary. The first two separated, one on each of side of the road, but one slightly in front of the other. They both crouched down. Then the next two quickly ran about eight yards in front of the other two and crouched. There was now one within a few feet from us. He was the one with headphones and carrying the radio control box on his back. I could hear a voice coming from his big bulky headphones but not clearly enough to hear what was being said. I'd seen many such patrols walk pass me before but none that had sprung from nowhere like this. On previous occasions I'd look closely at what they were wearing and at their faces — often one soldier would wink at me or smile or give me the thumbs-up. On this occasion, the soldier with the radio didn't even look at me or any of the three of us; he looked very serious and was obviously listening for instructions. The last pair ran in front of the middle pair, again about a further eight yards, and crouched too. The scene was like a film as all bystanders, including us, froze and gawked. I'd heard plenty of stories and headlines about the IRA firing at soldier patrols such as this — they were like sitting ducks without any real cover. I knew too that that civilians were often caught up in such incidents and shot, some fatally. I guess everyone else on the street had heard these stories too which explained the tsunami of anxiety and fear that swept across everyone's faces. People suddenly started darting into the chemist's, the butcher's, the fruit and veg shop and the bank, though this wasn't about getting some retail therapy or saving money. I faintly heard Val's voice say weakly, something like we should go back home, but she didn't know what to do, so we remained still, like remote figures on the island in the middle of the road crossing. We were good at being still when we played 'One, Two, Three Red Lights'. This was no game though.

Once all six soldiers seemed to be in their pre-arranged positions, the jeep spun off. The one at the tail motioned for traffic that had also frozen for a brief time to continue moving. Val took the chance to run across the road before the traffic reached us. She hadn't warned us and so just yanked me and Paul's hand. I did me best not to fall over as me sandals weren't the best footwear for sprinting. We ran to the bus stop but Val swerved us into the sweet shop that lay facing it. She wasn't ready to keep us out in the open.

Harry, the sweet shop owner, was at the window looking out along with four or five others who'd escaped from the Western Front. I stood looking at the Midget Gems, the Brandy Balls, the Lemon Bon Bons, the Dolly Mixtures, the Mars bars, the Fudge bars and all the glorious colours that surrounded the shop's walls. I had a moment of escapism from the drama outside, but then could hear the variety of 'radio' voices of the adults that bounced off the shop window, reverberated around the shop's walls, and stole me focus from the sugar-filled treats:

"What's goin' on now?"

"The traffic's moving freely now."

"I can see him there listening on his radio, something's going on."

"I wonder what it's all about?"

"All six of them boys are still down on their haunches."

"Oh God, I hope there's no bomb lurkin' somewhere."

"I need to get home to Gerry and me wains before something happens."

"Now, now, Mrs Ferguson, it'll be all right."

"You never know with these things, Mr Burke. Only last week Gerry himsel' got caught up with that bomb outside the Strand Road barracks. The car bomb went off only yards up from where he was standing."

"There's the bus, let's go, Ronnie. Let's get on it and away from here."

Val didn't hesitate either, and yanked me and Paul out of the door towards the now stationary bus. There was a sudden rush of bodies towards the safety of the bus's folding doors. I always got excited when on a bus as it was a rare occurrence — almost all of me journeys were either on foot or in Da's car. I didn't know if the shakiness in me body was excitement or anxiety from seeing the soldiers or others' reactions to them, or a mixture of both. Me head was in a spin. The image in me head was like a huge blurry cloud of pick and mix; sweets, chocolates, soldiers, Mrs Ferguson, a car exploding, a massive black puff of smoke, traffic lights, frozen bodies crossing the street, rifles, Mr Burke and black-and-white-spotted puppies. Out of the blur came a tall darkly-clad man with a machine in his hand. The bus conductor. At first, he reminded me of the scary man who always appeared at the side of me bunk bed and scared the life out of me. His smile changed that thought. It's amazing how a friendly smile can wash away fear and tension — well, reduce it anyway. Val gave him our fares. I watched him turn the handle on the ticket machine and then the magic happened — three brown-coloured tickets came spewing out like the white dove that would fly out of the magician's cupped hands. I wanted to hold me ticket like a grown-up but Val wanted to keep them safe in case an inspector got on and checked us for tickets.

Within minutes the bus was pretty full, there were only a couple of seats left. I could feel the atmosphere though, a real mixture of relief and fear. We were all on the bus, but the soldiers were still outside. The noise added to the atmosphere — anxious mouths spat out anxious words with a rattle, just like the conductor's ticket machine. Then the engine stopped making its rumbling racket that could barely be heard above the voices' rattle. Silence. Me heart beat faster again. I looked down the aisle of the bus and saw that two

217

soldiers had made an entrance. They held their rifles across their chests but their fingers close to the triggers. I hadn't even seen them move from their crouched positions on the street. No one spoke. The soldiers didn't speak. Everyone watched as they slowly made their way up the bus, checking everyone's face, looking at what people had on their laps, glancing under seats. They wore the serious face that soldiers always had when going into battle with the Germans. We weren't Germans, so why have this face? I was just about to ask Val what they were doing when she had pre-empted me and abruptly hushed me up before I could get a word out. No one spoke during the whole manoeuvre, until they got off and the bus re-started its journey to the Derry side. Conversations broke out but I couldn't make out any of them. I asked Val what all that was about, but she just said she didn't know and instead distracted us by talking about the *101 Dalmatians*. I learned that there were one hundred and one puppies and a nasty woman was trying to steal them. I didn't want to hear any more than that. I never liked to hear too much about something I was about to watch as it would spoil me enjoyment. The same is very true to this day, although it's much more difficult to not have more insight to a film or a telly drama or a novel in 2020. We're now constantly bombarded with adverts, trailers and video clips to spoil our fun of watching something in a state of pure innocence and ignorance.

Before I knew it, we were over the Craigavon

Bridge and at the top of Carlisle Road — our stop. As the bus slowed down to pull in, I could see Allen's clothes shop where Da bought our school uniforms from. I recalled the smell, the stuffiness of the clothes, Mr Allen with his tape measure round his neck and Da's embarrassing bartering over the cost. Then, of course, was Ma's red face of embarrassment — she hated Da's bargaining trait; we all did.

The last juddering brake of the bus brought me back to the present. I knew where the Rialto pictures was — through Derry's Walls via Ferryquay Gate and down to the right onto Market Street. I felt as if I'd walked all the streets of Derry with Da when out shopping with him on Saturday mornings — in all weathers. I could have started Google maps if only I'd known what we'd all come to rely on years later. I also knew we'd have to go through the pedestrian security gate that had been set up by the RUC and the army. As usual, there was a queue to get through the archway. Every man and woman had to go through a body search — legs apart and arms out wide. Any shopping or handbags had to be opened and looked at with prying fingers. Nobody spoke during these searches. Children were always quickly hushed by their accompanying adult, by a quick shout or a brisk slap — Da preferred the latter. It was always the RUC personnel who did the searching, with army reinforcements spread out on both sides of the archway. There was always one radio controller and at least four others, either standing or crouched with their rifles at the ready. We waited in the queue in silence. I was used to being silent, I had plenty of practice: in school, in Sunday school, in church, when adults visited the house, when the news was on the telly or radio, when having me haircut, when the football results were announced on the telly, and mostly in Da's company unless it was really obvious that he was in a light-hearted mood.

It was strange waiting with Val on this occasion. I hadn't done this with her in charge before. I was also tenser. Val didn't have Da's strength and also felt anxious herself, whereas Da was always fairly relaxed. He was never fazed by the Troubles, the bombings, the streets where riots took place. He felt comfortable wherever he walked in Derry, and he knew the place as if he'd been born there. So being with him during the search queues wasn't a problem in general. He also didn't have anything to hide, wasn't involved in any sectarian organisation (the Freemasons didn't count), wasn't carrying a gun and wasn't on any security list! He also looked natural when in these queues, whereas people who hated the security forces, the army and anyone who represented the British government couldn't hide their issues. I could see the hatred in their stares and hardened, gritted faces. I'm sure the police officers and the soldiers could see and feel this hatred boring into their souls. It was like a battle of determined faces, no one willing to give an inch. It created, though, a tension that only raw hatred can give birth to.

The queue this time was really long and we shuffled forward inch by inch. I had seen pictures on the telly of American prisoners of war during the Vietnam War, shuffling along in single file with their heads bowed, their bodies half the weight they had been when they first volunteered or drafted. They looked as if they were halfway to their deaths — I later discovered that that was often the outcome. We weren't heading towards our death, but there was still an air of death as we shuffled — one enemy with its uniforms and guns controlling the other. I also only knew too well that an outbreak of gunfire or a bomb going off could happen at any time. I just wanted to get to the Rialto, get inside and feel safe.

It was now our turn. Val pushed us forward in front of her so she could see us and to make sure we didn't misbehave. As it was summer and we weren't wearing coats, I knew that me and Paul wouldn't get searched. In the winter we'd get a brief body search on our bodies to make sure we didn't have a gun or carrying any explosives under our coats. The police officers didn't know us from sons of an IRA man, so we'd be treated with the same rudimentary caution. We were waved through the archway which always appeared like an endless tunnel even though it was a mere twenty-five feet long. Soldiers' suspicious stares greeted us at the other end with their fingers on their rifles and their berets tilted to one side. We stood motionless as Val had her handbag searched. She too had the same stare off the soldiers. She grabbed our hands and off we sped down the hill. None of us looked back.

Stop. Another queue! Oh no, there was a queue along the wall leading from the Rialto. There was a handful of grown-ups and about a dozen kids just like us itching to get inside. I didn't feel nervous at first but as we waited for the doors to open, I could feel eyes of some of the other boys on me and Paul. It was often believed in Derry that a Protestant could recognise a Catholic by how they looked and dressed, and vice versa. I knew they were Catholics and they knew we were Protestants. I didn't envisage a fight or anything, but if Val hadn't been with us, there might well have been. Their facial expressions weren't filled with the same hatred as the soldiers and the police, but there was definitely an antipathy that oozed from their stares. I did what I usually did on such occasions and kept me eyes to the ground; the aggression of boy gang mentality was often triggered by eye contact. If I wasn't looking at them then it didn't give the 'other' the excuse to accusingly ask what I was staring at. The aggression was then often contained. I also knew too well that boys would give any kind of aggro if they were bored. With relief, the doors opened and all sense of boredom, aggression, hatred and anxiety was swept away by the popcorn-smelling air that was sucked out by the doors. All kids focused on the excitement of sweets, Coke and popcorn to see us through the film.

Val had the money but we could choose what drink to have and what sweets to have. Me and Paul had sixpence each to spend. Coca Cola was our definite choice of drink as we never had it at home. The popcorn didn't look appealing despite all those American kids eating it on the telly. So packets of Poppets and Revels were chosen to be washed down by the fizzy sugary blackness of Coca Cola. These chocolates might not seem a big deal, but as we were rarely bought them, they were a real treat. Then Val handed an entrance ticket to me. It was real. I could feel me body jump around on the inside — and that was even before the sugar rush of the chocolates and Coca Cola.

The auditorium was unbelievable. Huge red, soft seats were spread out in rows, each with its arms. The screen was still white but seemed hundreds of times bigger than our telly screen. The Revels were gone before the film started but me eyes were in shock once the lights went off and the screen lit up — it was in colour! Val hadn't told us about this; she'd kept it as a surprise. It was just the Dalmatians that were still in black and white! Before I knew it, it was time for the interval (time to change the reel Val said). It gave me the chance to eat me Poppets as I'd been so encapsulated by the film, I'd forgotten all about them. Me and Paul must have talked through the whole first reel again while we waited for the film to restart. The second reel was even more frantic than the first, and filled with more tension than I could bear. It was such a relief to see baddie, red-lipped Cruella de Vil get her comeuppance. Even though tense films usually ended like this, I would never bank on it and therefore, like most viewers, I'd go through the torture of thinking the baddie might win and the goodie die. Even as an adult many years later, I wouldn't allow meself to assume that all evil would be dealt the deadly blow as part of a film's denouement — the director's skill no doubt.

Getting outside once again was weird. Me mind was still focused on the big screen and in a world full of black and white spotted puppies, yet me eyes saw the outside world cut in half; the top half was blindingly bright by the sun's rays, but the bottom half was coldly cool by the greyness of Derry's Walls. It took some time to re-adjust me vision and me head. The journey home was straightforward compared to the journey from home earlier — I barely remember the walk down to Foyle Street to catch the bus, the bus journey itself and the walk from Bond's Hill to the house. I guess me energy reserves had been well and truly used up with all shenanigans of the day's trip to the pictures. Telling Ma all about the trip was all over in seconds as I just blurted out what happened at the end to Cruella de Vil. Ma would have been disappointed as most parents would be at such times, when their offspring appeared selfish and inconsiderate and were only interested in playing with their friends, rather than showing gratitude or giving thanks. Ma, as I soon learned meself when a parent, accepted that this was the way things were, and didn't show any disappointment. She would have been used to similar responses to all her offspring when asked typical questions, such as the one parents just can't seem to avoid asking — 'How was school today?' Val might have taken a bit longer to accept me seeming ingratitude, but didn't show it either. No two trips to the pictures are the same, but as is often the case, the maiden voyage will last forever.

# Chapter 11
# Me and Paul, the Twins

With me older siblings, specific events stand out in me memory, but with me twin brother Paul, nothing really specific stands out. This is not doing him any disservice, but a reflection that we spent so much time together doing things, that memories with him are more habitual, uneventful, minor, daily or 'everyday' events that their totality is what makes memories of him memorable.

It's funny that the memories of conflict with him seem to rest more in our early teens — after we'd vacated the Four Streets, rather than when we lived in them. I'm sure Ma, Da and me sisters would have different views on that. What Ma did recall on numerous occasions, during family gatherings over the years, was how I was the 'ringleader'. This labelling referred to those times when something was broken, or when one of us was hurt, or when we broke 'the rules'. Paul was seen as the more placid and passive of the two of us, whilst I was the energetic, creative, curious and mischievous one. Don't get me wrong, I was far from being a rebel; fear of reprisals and punishment dampened any of the Fidel Castro that may have lain within me skinny frame. But I wore the Castro 'badge' when compared to Paul. Trial by Ma and Da's jury left me as the main instigator and therefore more guilty of any offence than me five-minutes-older twin brother.

Let's start with the playpen (though I did give it a mention earlier). Now, from our early days as wee toddlers, I was clearly the skinny twin and Paul the chubby one. I don't know if this was a genetic circumstance, but we were definitely fed the same bottles of formula milk. As far as I've been told, I didn't drink any fewer ounces at feeding times, but our body weights were clearly at odds by our first birthday! By the time we were twenty-four months old, it would have been typical of me older siblings to make fun at the fact that we looked so different and quizzed if we were indeed brothers. The dimple on our chins was the only discernible true likeness to counter such jokes. Paul's dark hair and me own blonde hair was also established along with his flat boxer-like nose and my Roman pointed one — so there was marked evidence for such jesting. However, we were the same age and needed the same nurturing and containment. So, being put in the blue wooden playpen in the middle of the kitchen for a bit, was a daily activity for us so that Ma could get on with her mammoth-long daily To Do list. I certainly wouldn't criticise her for leaving us in there for lengthy periods or putting us in there beyond the age that we had outgrown it; how else was a housewife and a mother of seven children that included a pair of twenty-month-old boys meant to cook, bake, clean, wash and more, with us two running around her ankles? Toys to keep us occupied were few and far between; wooden cars, noisy rattles, teething rings and a handful of colourful figures and shapes made from wool (that were hand-knitted by Ma and me sisters) was our stockpile of stimuli. Of course, there was no television in the background either, apart from *Watch with Mother*, and that only lasted twenty minutes. I could never understand the 'with' bit in the title. No mother in her right mind would sit down with her child or children when this programme was on; they'd take advantage of not having to keep an eye on the wain(s) and be off catching up with chores or having a cigarette with a cuppa or a quick 'romantic' fumble with their unemployed hubby. Ma would have done chores — she didn't smoke and Da was at work! She barely took a tea break at any time of day. In fact, parents of Ma and Da's generation and social position didn't have the cultural mindset of spending time to nurture child development that became more commonplace with parents of the new millennia. Saying that, Derry in the sixties had families of a considerable size and therefore proactively stimulating a child's physical, mental and emotional development was not high in a parent's priority — Ma was no exception. Parents like Ma and Da left any form of education to the school system, with the exception of religious education that was primarily left to the Church, of course. The fact that six of me parents' children passed the eleven-plus exam said a great deal about the education system rather

228

than their own tutelage endeavours.

We can all acknowledge that a child (never mind an adult) can get bored without some form of stimulation. I would get bored more readily than Paul and therefore would dismiss the various wood and wool-designed shapes well before he would. It was no surprise then that me brain would find its own style of stimulation, often at the expense of me fatter twin brother. I had already paid the price on numerous occasions of messing with Paul by taunting him with pokes, pinches, and punches. His extra body weight brought extra power and force — and therefore greater pain for me. You'd think I'd learn me lesson, but retribution and retaliation wasn't enough to quench boredom's thirst, so I would always go back for more! Then one day I made a discovery.

The playpen wasn't fixed to anything and therefore was prone to being moved about the lino floor of the kitchen as me and Paul bashed into it and shook it about. Ma would come in from the scullery at intervals to check on us and pull it back to the centre of the room. I can see now why she did. On this particular day, Ma had got more distracted by her chores and didn't stick her head round the scullery door for a lengthier time than usual. The playpen had inched its way to rest on the red leather sofa (it was never referred to as a chaise longue, despite its resemblance). I tried to get me knee unto the seat of it but was a couple of inches short. I needed something to stand on. An over-stuffed, hand-knitted doll that had been handed down from me sisters was just the prop I needed. Although me tiny body weight meant that I sunk into it a bit, there was enough stuffing to give me the extra two inches that I needed to get me knee up. Paul watched in amazement as I was up and over the wooden frame and 'free'. He tried to copy me but his greater weight meant that he sunk more deeply into the doll and therefore had less of a lift. He swung his chubby knee up to reach the seat, and it merely kissed its red leather upholstery. I watched as he tried and tried to pull up his round frame but he couldn't manage it. There can be a sense of self-fulfilment and of an endorsement of one's narcissistic tendencies to have another human being copy what you do, follow the path of following you and look up to you as the superior being. Paul gave me this from an early age — different personalities present, I guess. On this occasion, my ego was aptly fed by the fact that Paul had tried to copy me, but then it gorged on the fact that he had failed miserably. I became William Golding's Jack, welcoming the power and authority that had been part-granted and part-taken. I circled the pen, Paul ran to wherever I rested. I reached out as if to help him, as Ma would do to show she was about lift him up. This time though, he didn't receive an embrace. Instead, he was met with an ear being pulled. He didn't learn his lesson the first time, nor the second, nor the third — nor the sixth. My belly of pleasure wasn't satiated by the infliction of pain on me twin, but more with the power

I had over him. I had freedom of movement; he was trapped. I think I was oblivious to any pain being experienced until he started to cry. He didn't inherit Ma's stoicism and therefore didn't necessarily cry, but bawled loudly! Me pathetic attempt at getting him to stop was to pull his ears again — wrong move. Ma had come in from the scullery and caught me with me fingers on me right hand firmly holding on to Paul's left ear. I had barely released me grip when she swung her strong right hand and smacked me hard on me bare leg. I didn't understand the exact 'words' but I definitely understood their meaning. Two further smacks made sure that there wasn't any likelihood of me not understanding. Now I knew what pain was, as if I hadn't known before! Tears came to match Paul's. Cries came to match his too. It was years of being smacked by Ma and Da before I taught meself to hold back the tears and to hold back expressions of pain — another of life's power battles! Still crying, Ma picked me up and put me back in the pen. She then placed our dummies in our mouths to stem the noise — it had an immediate effect. It's difficult to cry with a dummy in your mouth, yet it's also difficult not to suck on a dummy that's similar to that which you had been accustomed to sucking on to get milk from the bottle! We watched Ma move the pen away from the sofa and place a chair between them so my heroics couldn't be repeated. She parted the scene with a frown and a pointing of her index finger, both aimed at me. Another lesson learned, so I thought.

There were clearly many incidents involving me and Paul that led to some kind of reprimand, punishment, scolding or beating — at times from Ma, at times from Da and at times from both of them. The list is endless, but the determined common denominator was that I was at the root, the instigator, the over-curious one, the leader, the one with the devilment in him, the one who wasn't content to keep still. I was to blame! We all know that once you've been handed a label, been branded, got a stigma — it's almost impossible to erase it from others' minds, others' perspectives, others' interpretation. So, I wasn't an exception. It didn't bother me too much most of the time as I was usually the one with the ideas and would push the boundaries of house rules, Da's rules, Ma's rules, the Church's rules and me culture's rules more than Paul. It was when I was truly innocent about something going missing or something being broken or not being in the vicinity of a wrongdoing, that I would rage. Me rage would lead me to speak me mind and stand up for justice and me innocence, but what was me own tiny voice in the midst of all the powerful rules? It was either not heard at all or so poorly heard that it was deemed defiance in the wake of the rules laid down by whoever. Ultimately, 'fitting' retribution followed. The most significant incidents that trickle from the caverns of me memory are the 'fishing in the Foyle', the 'tittering over of the telly', the 'chipping of the china wall plate' and the 'freeing of the fat-bellied pig and her piglets'.

A number of boys would congregate by the sewage pipe that poked out of the ground beyond the bowels of the railway line — that lay just beyond the Tins. They'd have a foot-long piece of wood with fishing gut wrapped around its centre and a hook knotted on the end of the gut. No one fished properly with fishing rods in the Four Streets — at least not in the sewage-filled and murky waters of the River Foyle. None of the boys in the Four Streets could afford such a pastime's gear anyway, so reverting to primitive basics was what they did. Me and Paul didn't fish at all — that was one risk too far! What we did though, was dig for worms over the Tins to give to the bigger boys who fished. The pleasure we got from mixing a bit of washing up liquid with water and pouring it over the muddy surface of our own Windsor Park to then watch the worms squirming their way out of the earth to avoid intoxication far outweighed standing precariously on the sewage pipe with a bit of stick with gut and a hook. The worms were easy pickings and it wouldn't be long before we'd get a discarded bean can, full of the wriggling invertebrates. The fatter and longer they were, the more we revelled in collecting them, as we'd get praise from the bigger boys. We did, of course, select a few to keep so that we could chop off either end, just to see how the separated parts frantically wriggled about in probable pain in search of continual life. I could only stomach the sight for so long before flashes of dismembered bodies from post-car bomb scenes splashed on the telly's news would shock me into ending the sickening torture of the worms. Well, till the next time.

Supplying the bigger boys with worms gave me and Paul street credit that all younger boys craved. We'd then sit on the cobbled, angled wall that was built to support the railway track and act as the bank of the river. Watching the bigger boys balance themselves as they walked on the sewage pipe so that they were a few feet away from the bank and were flanked by the dirty water brought both fear and admiration to me. How could they not slip and fall in? We were both offered the lines a few times but always refused on the grounds that Da would kill us if 'anything happened'.

Then one day Paul slipped as he made his way back up the cobbled bank. The stocky Tom Ferguson caught him by the arm but his left foot went into the water, soaking his sock and shoe. I suggested we sit it out in the Tins whilst the wet gear dried out but Paul wouldn't agree so he headed home. I knew it wouldn't be long before I was summoned to face the music and the inevitable telling- off. Ma's finger was at work again — at both of us, but I knew she thought it was me who had taken Paul down to the forbidden river. I knew too that she'd eventually say the words, "Wait till your father gets home". Da rarely differentiated between us when it came to blame — we were both there so we were both in the wrong — whack. Berating Paul for going home and confessing was a waste of time — he'd just stand there in silence and take it. I'm not sure what frustrated me the most, the confession or the lack of reasoning behind the confession.

The telly and the china plate incidents both took place in the hub of the kitchen. Neither were major in any capacity but they were both stories that Ma would repeatedly retell throughout me life, to family, friends, relatives and neighbours. Once these memories were triggered by some word or recollection or the like, she'd be off retelling. Although me and Paul were both partners in crime, I was the clearly the protagonist.

I liked to sit on the chair that was merely two and a half feet away from the telly — a habit that was probably responsible for me hating bright lights and the sun's glare in older years. We were about five and it was during the eight-week summer holidays. We'd just finished watching Bill and Ben, the flowerpot men. I didn't want to watch the Test Card that came on once the programme was over. That silly girl playing Noughts and Crosses whilst the clown stood doing nothing, whilst boring jingly brass instruments, reminiscent of fairground carousels, played in the background. So, I thought I'd push the telly back away from me. I couldn't budge the heavy brute of the telly so Paul joined in to help. The task now was all about defeating the stubborn telly, and nothing to do with the picture or the music. Ma appeared just as we managed to move it. However, to all our horror, the telly which had been soundly balanced on the high square table, was now tipping the table forwards and the telly itself backwards. We watched in slow motion (things falling always seem to take on that slow moving effect) as the telly fell on its back and dropped a foot before becoming wedged between the cornered wall and shelf of the table. Moving either item would result in the other falling completely to the hard lino floor. There was no need to guess that this evidence was going to be left for Da's return — a whole three hours! Of course, Ma tried to get to the bottom of the misdemeanour and Paul duly obliged by pointing at me and saying that I'd started it. There was no need for the jury to leave the kitchen to decide on their verdict of guilty. No finger- pointing this time — two quick slaps on the legs this time. The sting lasted a while but I knew that there were greater stings to come once Da got back. I couldn't have managed the sin without Paul but I can confess that I was the greater of the two sinners on this occasion.

I was the greater of the two sinners again when it came to the china wall plate. This three-dimensional piece of crockery was fashionable in many households I'd been in — me granny's, me aunties', me neighbours', Da's Donegal relatives. Rural folk and city folk had them. They'd often depict a country scene. Ours showed a cobble-stoned village bridge with a river flowing through its arches in the foreground, old thatched cottages with wooden criss-cross beams signalling their frames surrounding them, and a village church on a hill in the background. A sickly yellow was the main colour. It was the only ornament or picture or photograph that was hung up in the kitchen and was placed dead centre in the wall that the sofa ran along. It clearly clashed with the psychedelic wallpaper that was typical in sixties homes; a mix of yellow, brown, white and cream circles and oblong shapes that were confined within squares that had their corners cut off. At least I was spared the traditional three ducks that seemed to also be on the walls of almost every house I went into. No one ever commented on the plate and there appeared no history or sentimentality attached to it — it was just something to fill the space on the wall.

It was post-teatime and therefore post-news time. The house had gone through its customary silence so that Da could hear every syllable uttered by Ian Paisley and John Hume. Even *Gunfight at the OK Coral* had old adversaries Wyatt Earp and John 'Doc' Holliday put aside their history and join forces to fight on the same side, but Paisley and Hume had daily gunfights on our television screens — firing the same bullets, from the same guns, from the same holsters. The outcomes were also the same — one trying to out-shout the other with the same biased ferocity until the neutral BBC 'referee' rang the bell for the cameraman to stop filming! It's no wonder that me tolerance for difference and diversity grew from an early age. It was hard going, having to endure the likes of Paisley and Hume, each in their own bubble on the telly, and Da outside the telly in *his* own bubble looking into theirs.

By the time the news was truly over, well, till the

next dose at nine o'clock anyway, me and Paul were beside ourselves with boredom, energy to burn and the desire to let off some steam. So, when *Top of the Pops* started and the atmosphere was full of positivity amongst me sisters, who watched the programme each week with utter longing and anticipation, me and Paul were ready to rock. We'd heard Mungo Jerry's 'In the Summertime' over and over as it stayed for weeks at number one and, of course, was on each week. It also had a real catchy beat and melody to it. It clearly helped release the trapped energy that had generated during the silence at news time. Me and Paul would sometimes get our prize tennis racquets bought from the posh department store (with its escalator that I'd only seen on telly before) on a trip to Belfast. The Woolworths racquets came years later. We'd stand proudly on the sofa strumming to whatever was on the pop show. Well, we didn't necessarily stand, but jump up and down to the rhythm of the beat — unless Da was around to ensure our feet didn't move an inch above the red leather and the springs below weren't tested for their durability. Strumming was great but me fascination of percussion and an innate urge to drum, rose up inside me. I think there is clearly something primitive in boys and men to beat a drum; from pipe bands to rock bands, from Apaches to Mayans, from the bodhran to the lambeg drum, the beating of wood on skin is a central dimension of ceremonies, celebrations, war, and undoubtedly, representations of masculinity. I would always find, and still do, me fingers voluntarily tapping away at some sound in me head or being played out around me. Driving me car and listening to me CD collection would have me constantly giving the steering wheel a good old battering. I wouldn't be alone though; there would be countless other men doing likewise — I'd very rarely see women doing the same.

So, I dropped me makeshift guitar and went out to the scullery to get one of ma's wooden spoons. I knew where they were as I'd often use them to mix her cake or bread ingredients for her. Ma saw me but didn't quiz me. By the time she came into the kitchen to check on what I was using the spoons for, I'd chipped away at the bottom of the ornamental plate — about three inches in length. There were no cracks or huge damage done, but there was enough to warrant a hard slap on me legs and a sharp-edged tongue lash at me sisters for not paying attention to what I was doing. I was caught in the act by Ma again. Paul wasn't the victim this time, but was still the innocent-looking one of the two of us. The plate remained on that wall for the next few years. It was then hung on the kitchen wall of the new house that Ma lived in till she passed away, for forty-four years. Ma loved to tell this story (like many others), but I always thought, and didn't share this thought, that the damage wasn't that bad or it wouldn't have been hung for all those years later. None of me siblings were the least interested in having it when we discussed what personal possessions we'd like to have of Ma's, after her passing, and couldn't fathom me own desire to have it. It now hangs proudly on the wall of the spare room in me own house now. Smoothing me fingers over its chipped edge, takes me right back in time.

The next incident that involved me and Paul and where I came out as the instigator of bad fortune, was the venturing into unpermitted territory and then being superfluously being grassed on by Mrs 'Nosey' Hegarty, who lived across the street. All parents stipulate geographical boundaries that are supposed to create greater safety for their children — of course, the Troubles added to these restrictions for me and Paul. We weren't necessarily banned from going as far as the Waterside Railway Station. It was just beyond the coal yard, which lay adjacent to the Four Streets. It only seemed a stone's throw away when I stood on top of the sleepers. It always felt odd when I was only slightly beyond familiar territory, yet felt the fear of the unfamiliar. I was used to seeing the station from inside Da's car, or being on the bus with Ma or walking down Duke Street to visit the hardware shop with Da. Of course, I was there every year to get the train for the Sunday school excursion. It was also only a stroll away from Lucas' sweet shop on Bond's Hill, one of the many sweet shops within a five-minute radius from me house, that sold black and red liquorice strings as long as me arms. Yet, when I went even twenty yards beyond the shop or through the gap in the wall that bordered York Street, and from where I could throw a stone at the coal yard's gate, I felt very uneasy. I felt immediate danger and an acute sense of the unknown. I didn't know this alien environment or the people or kids who lived in the row of a dozen houses that ran along the coal yard. It's strange that being in an unknown environment when an adult can often have one of two impacts — one of fear of the unknown or one of excitement and adventure through exploration.

On this particular day, a Saturday in April, me, Paul, Jimmy, Aidan and Derek ended up in the York Street back lane. This lane usually felt the safest of the five lanes of the Four Streets; it wasn't hemmed in by the backyards of houses and didn't have the army barracks with its lookout posts bearing down on your every movement. There was also only one dog that lived on that side of the street and that would threaten to rip your throat out if you ventured near its gate. This was in sharp contrast to other lanes where half a dozen dogs lurked menacingly behind well-bolted wooden gates. We'd replayed the Chelsea versus Leeds Utd cup final from the Saturday before, over and over again, earlier in the week and earlier in the day, so playing football wasn't an option for us. Not playing football often left us a bit bored, and this occasion was no different. We came to the gaping hole in the two-foot-thick grey wall. No one had any idea how this was created — no road led up to it for a car to hit it and so start the dismantling process. In fact, it resembled more of something from *Colditz* or *The Great Escape*, with its irregular shape that allowed only small frames to get through it. We thought we'd play prisoners of war. We had to go through the gap to start the journey to reach our beloved homeland and beloved families who hadn't seen us or had a letter from us for months. No one wanted to go first so we ended up 'drawing sticks'. Jimmy was the oldest by two months so he held the five sticks, cupped between his two hands, without showing their lengths. I drew the second and it was shorter than the first. I knew my fate was sealed; when we played this game, the one who held the sticks also gathered them and would ensure that most of the sticks were of near-equal length apart from the shortest. I had to wait till the others drew theirs to have me fate confirmed — Jimmy's stick did that. So, I had to venture through the wall first. I kept telling meself it was only a wall and that I could clearly see that there was nothing on the other side to be scared of. The nine houses that lined the right of me showed no activity, whilst on the left, there was a fifteen-foot wall that bordered a timber yard. As it was a Saturday, there was no life nor sound coming from it. I was scared. I had gone through the wall before a couple of times and was scared then too, but the other side still felt unfamiliar and alien. There was also an eerie silence. The small street was protected from any traffic sounds, there wasn't a train on the nearby lines, the coal yard was closed for the weekend, and there was a suffocating heat that bounced off the tarmac.

"Get on wee ye."

"Scaredy cat."

"Chicken face."

"Need your mammy."

These words all rang in me ears from the others. I had to do it before I was totally crucified, so in I crawled, pretending to escape the German POW camp. I crouched down like the soldiers I watched both on the telly and on the streets of Derry, but had no imaginary rifle in me hands this time — I was an escapee. I signalled to the others to follow me as I crept along under the windows of the houses on the right. Paul followed next. We couldn't be spotted or we'd be turned in. When we got to the end of the street, we headed down Brae's Hill to the gates of the coal yard, and then turned left. Well, we could only turn left as the coal yard was in front of us and to the right. I stopped dead. I could see three older boys up ahead standing outside one of the dozen houses. I didn't recognise them so I knew that there may be an issue. Boys never like any other boys in their turf, but if there was a classified difference in religion between you and the other boys, this heightened tensions and increased the possibility of a bit of eye-balling and a confrontation — or a kicking. I'd never had a kicking or had reason to give anyone else one either, but I knew plenty of Protestant boys who went out of their way to give a Catholic boy a kicking. Then again, they were the same boys who would get a kicking from Catholics if the occasion arose. I kept to me own rule that if I didn't seek conflict then I wouldn't be dragged into it by others.

We kept to the coal yard side of the road — to be opposite the other boys. The three boys glared at us. It was difficult not to even look at them but I made fleeting glances to check if they moved from the doorstep and in case we had to make a run for it. I was a quick sprinter and knew I'd probably get away, but Paul wasn't. I whispered to him to walk quicker and in front, but instead he ran. His movement triggered all of us to run. When I slowed down when I knew I was safe, I could hear the other boys laughing their heads off to see us run with fear. I felt stupid for running but also relieved that nothing had happened. Paul got stick for running in the first place, but on this occasion, I didn't chip in — I knew he ran because of his slowness. The running quickly brought us to the railway station. Jimmy and Aidan wanted to go inside the station but me and Paul knew this was too risky for fear of being spotted by someone who knew us and might tell Ma and Da that they'd seen us there — we'd only get a hiding. Derek also didn't want to be spotted so we agreed to bypass it.

Isn't it strange how we react when we see something but at a different time to when we would normally see it, or are placed somewhere that we have been before but at a different time? We can feel misplaced or confused or alien to the previous experiences. That's how I felt when we ambled past the station with its square clock tower and proud black and white faces pointing to all four compass points. I never paid any attention to the clock when being there for the annual Sunday school excursion to Portrush. I also never noticed the perfectly formed, grey block walls that guarded the now diesel, but formerly, steam trains from potential non-paying travellers. The olive-green, slanted tiled roof also passed me by. I guess I was too focused on what was going on at eye level, with the crowds of people who belonged to the church, but were not all churchgoers. Of course, there was the high level of excitement of the once-a-year trip on a train, with its long corridor that ran the length of each carriage and the actual carriage that would house us Kennedys and another family or two. Everything seemed huge. I didn't think of the excursion as we sauntered past it, just focused on me lack of emotional connection and sense of unfamiliarity to a building that once a year was the meeting and end point to a fantastic day out to the seaside on a train, I didn't belong here at this moment.

We were now on Duke Street and me feeling of not belonging was overtaken by feeling very vulnerable. We were in quite an open space and prone to being spotted by a nosey neighbour who could grass us up, so we decided to head towards the river.

Duke Street led to Craigavon Bridge and seeing it highlighted that we were clearly beyond the boundaries permitted by Ma and Da. There was building work going on. A number of old shops and houses had already been demolished to make way for a brand-new carriageway. I had no idea what a carriageway looked like, but it sounded like a big road of some kind. The road builders had also started to eat into the River Foyle as steel girders stuck out of it in preparation to widen Duke Street for the new road. Rows of railway sleepers had been placed to create a temporary walkway to allow access to the water's edge and the steel girders. A number of plant vehicles were sleeping after being put to bed for the weekend and created a screen from car drivers, bus drivers and shoppers. This was the perfect spot to hang out away from the 'searching Germans'. The building work created an endless supply of stones, pebbles, broken bricks and rocks for us to throw into the river. A tight crawl under the wired fencing led us to the sleepers. We had to make frequent trips back under the fence though to restock our supplies of throwing ammunition. One minute we were throwing pretend petrol bombs we'd seen rioters on the Falls Road do, the next we were Clint Eastwood in *Where Eagles Dare*, throwing grenades.

After a while we just sat with our legs hanging over the sleepers. I watched the dark and murky water below us slowly become more energetic and make louder splashing noises against the steel uprights. Me mind drifted back to me friend Mary who had fallen into the river and drowned a year ago — she was only eight. I thought about her struggling in this dirty water and about seeing her all dry, but colourless in the open coffin a couple of days later. I felt a sense of loss inside of me as I remembered the shock of her playing on the street one minute and gone forever the next. I guess the Troubles created that feeling for a lot of people. As I focused on the water, I became aware that the air seemed to be changing too. The sun had disappeared behind a blanket of greyness, but the clouds didn't look like they had rain hiding in them. We were all experts at reading the weather as our lives revolved checking and re-checking the skies for signs of rain. It wasn't just me and Paul who checked for rain approaching to see if we could play outside or not, or if we had to make our way nearer to the house for fear of being caught too far away when the heavens opened. Ma checked for the all-clear to hang out washing, or bring it in, and Da checked for rain to decide whether or not to wash the car or start on his favourite project of removing rust from the car sill. (Most men would be devastated to find a hole in their car, but Da was elated as it fed this pastime).

Rain wasn't pending, but something else was. We suddenly became aware of two helicopters shooting out from the barracks. I'd never seen them coming out from this angle before; they were normally just above me when coming out of the barracks, but this time they were more reminiscent of helicopters making their way through the Viet Cong jungle. They now looked more menacing. Noise behind us also became more evident — I could hear people's voices and vehicles that weren't your average car engine. Fear swept through all of us as we crept past the diggers and Caterpillars to the fence. Duke Street was now full of the RUC — grey jeeps and Saracens lined both sides. Something really bad was happening.

I'd heard snippets of conversations between Ma and Da and me uncles and aunties when we were at Drumalief the Sunday before, about bloody Catholics and their vermin ways — though this was not untypical rhetoric when at me granny's. Last Sunday was different as they said something about a civil march in Derry. I had no idea what 'civil' meant but was very aware what a march was; me childhood was full of them. I couldn't ask any questions as they only led to "don't worry your wee head about it". Adults never explained anything in detail to us kids so we were often left with a lack of knowing or understanding or just plain confusion. Instead, we only had their outspoken and prejudiced discriminatory opinions to catch hold of. Well, I say 'they'; it was always evident to me that Ma and Da weren't as vocal as Ma's more Protestant and Loyalist siblings and their partners.

As we crawled under the fence, Paul snagged his T-shirt on the shoulder and scraped his skin. The adrenalin-fuelled fear stopped any whinging or crying but we both knew that there would be an inquisition when we got back and definitely a few whacks from Da. Just what we didn't need I thought, but now wasn't the time to have a go at him. I could clearly see the police presence everywhere. Emerging from our bellies to get under the fence I could see that there were also loads of people to accompany the security forces. They had cameras like those I'd seen on *Football Focus*, so I knew they were telly ones. This was no football match. There were also a lot of people behind the police at the bottom of Bond's Hill. I wondered if Da was there as he'd often venture over to the outskirts of the Bogside on a Saturday or Sunday to see at first hand the rioting. I know Ma hated him going there for fear of getting 'caught up in it'.

A police officer with stripes on his sleeve saw us and with a serious frown across his face, waved his shiny truncheon in our faces and told us to get home as the march was on its way and this was no place for wee boys. We ran towards the station with our hearts beating with fear. However, as is often the case, adrenalin controlled our actions. We didn't head for home and instead headed for the high wall that ran along the station and the coal yard. Aidan was convinced that once on the wall we could make our way back to the bottom of York Street and away from the main road. I wasn't sure but gave in to the peer pressure from him and Jimmy.

The gaps in the wall where the mortar had broken off and where the odd stone block had crumbled gave us enough of a footing to get to the top of the wall. What a view it was from the top — Duke Street filled with RUC uniforms and their dull grey transport vehicles — dozens of them. I could then see the beginning of the march as bodies and banners made their way across Craigavon Bridge. Orange marches with their pipes, accordions, flutes and drums, announced their pending arrival long before they could be seen, but on this occasion, there was no noise, no sound — just an eerie feel. The marchers didn't march in lines and rows but were en masse across the road. It didn't seem right not seeing them in an orderly fashion like the bands and Orangemen. It felt different too, as if something bad might happen. I could make out a huge white banner with black writing being held by the marchers at the front as they turned off the bridge and unto Duke Street. I couldn't see what it said, but it again was different to the Orange Order or Apprentice Boys' banners that were held by pole bearers high into the air. There was no sound; it was more reminiscent of a sombre funeral march than a march I was used to seeing and hearing.

Paul was fearful now too and wanted to get back home to face the telling-off and the consequences of 'breaking the rules'. So we said we were going. Then there was a series of roars — from the people gathered at the foot of Bond's Hill and from the RUC. They launched at the marchers with whatever weapons they held in their hands and a battle took place. I could see people being beaten and hear their screams. The roaring and the shouting and the screams made me stomach sick and I felt faint. I never liked violence on any level and hated to see someone being physically hurt and bleeding as a consequence. Me and Paul made a quick exit along the wall and didn't stop to see any more. Only Aidan and Jimmy stayed, whilst the others followed us. The police officer was right; this wasn't a place for wee boys.

By the time we got to the bottom of York Street, our hands and arms and legs and clothes were filthy from the coal dust that had settled on the wall that surrounded the coal yard. We had a feeling of relief to be away from the trouble, but utter dread to get home — we knew we were for it. It didn't matter on this occasion that Mrs Hegarty had already told Da that she'd seen us around the station — our appearance was evidence enough. The telling-off was followed by the beating, that was followed by a bath, that was followed by being sent to bed before it was even teatime. No tea was brought up either. No sisters or brother appeared in the room either — we were in solitary confinement like Steve McQueen or John Wayne, but with each other for company. We didn't say much to each other anyway, so I was lost in me own thoughts of replaying the whole escapade from start to finish. I tried to avoid the images of the fighting and the beating of innocent people who were just marching for their own cause, whatever that was. I knew I'd have nightmares that night — I wasn't wrong.

In later years I learned the true history of that day, the terrible injustices that civil rights marchers endured and the huge inequality that existed by the very nature of what religion, never mind class, that you were born into. Me own feelings of inequality clearly mirrored those of many others — yet I was aware that me own

251

suffering at me da's hand of injustice was only a segment of that dished out to many others during the Troubles. Trying to remedy the chaos that suffering, killing, injustice and hatred brought by throwing futile fragments of order at it, was always going to be the proverbial sticking plaster on a massive incision of the flesh. Me and many others during the Troubles had to find ways of distracting ourselves from the chaos, but I guess it was easier for us kids — play was our saviour.

Me and Paul found play a real oasis of escapism. Being both boys and interested in sport and competition gave us the platform to find solace away from the tensions around us. Playing games when it was just the two of us would be devoid of religious bias and prejudice, devoid of fear of being judged as different by others and devoid of being bullied by older boys or even sisters. We had the traditional and structured games such as Mousetrap, Ludo, Snakes and Ladders, Trouble, Draughts, Risk, Tiddly Winks, Blow Football and Monopoly. There would also be a variety of playing card games like 'Three Anythings and an Ace', 'Sevens' and 'Trumps'. At times we'd play games with Hazel and Val (and even Da once in a while) but in general it was just the two of us. There was no doubting that we were fierce competitors but it rarely spilled over into big arguments or fights. We were also pretty good at changing the rules in order to make some games a bit more exciting. However, it was the games that we made up that showed off our creative ability. The space behind the sofa in the 'good' sitting room became our stadia, our gladiatorial arena, our western front. We'd make use of a whole range of bits and pieces from the board games — the die, the draught pieces, the Monopoly houses and hotels, the mice, the counters and the plastic football. Add our bag of marbles, our vast collection of small plastic cowboys and Indians and World War Two soldiers, a tennis ball, a washed-out jam jar, an empty cardboard box, and we had the components for games, fights, battles and ingenious competitions. At times it would be just me versus Paul in a one-to-one face-off of some kind. This might have meant Paul lining up his cowboys and me lining up me Indians opposite them — about one hundred men each. We'd then take turns to roll a marble to 'kill' the enemy by knocking them over. The dead would be placed to the side so as to create gaps and enhance the need for accuracy. We would create famous battles such as Little Bighorn and Wounded Knee and even rewrite the history of the United States according to who won the battles. Other times, we created a league or cup competition that included all the teams in the First Division at the time. We'd take turns to be a team and play out a match with points awarded for a win or draw. We'd even cut out the cardboard from a cornflakes packet to make trophies and cut strips so that we could write out the teams. Numbers were written on to tiny pieces of paper and Sellotaped to marbles. They were then placed in a sister's woolly hat. Teams were allocated a number and the marbles then drawn out one at a time as Saint and Greavsie did in *On the Ball*, when making the draw for each round of the FA Cup. Our games helped to disperse the boredom of Sundays and the constant periods of being trapped in the house by the incessant rain showers. Our games were also a great distraction from the bombs, the shootings, the killings, the gang warfare, the riots, the sirens and the helicopters. There was no telly or radio in the sitting room either, so we escaped the incessant reporting of each and every event that Da was so dearly obsessed with hearing about.

We couldn't escape the ingredients of the Troubles as much when we played outside, but this didn't stop our creative play. Living in the bottom house in the street gave us a huge gable wall to play against, whilst Da's wooden garage door was a perfect size for a goal. Our football skills were definitely honed on these two surfaces and our creative minds went to work to invent numerous games using a football in the main, but tennis balls, tennis racquets, bouncing sponge balls, cricket bats, chalk and a yellow-dot old squash ball found over the Tins were put to good use to satiate our thirst for competition and fantasy. Using our tennis racquets and a tennis ball to re-enact Jack Nicklaus' win at Pebble Beach was one of me favourite creations.

The road that ran along the bottom of the Four Streets was not in a good state of repair in 1972 — there was talk of a dual carriageway being built so the council weren't going to patch up the potholes or relay the road if it was going to be dug up in the near future. Me and Paul watched the US Open on the telly and were fascinated by the sport — one which we never experienced or even knew of anyone actually playing it. I didn't even know where a golf club existed in Derry, if at all. That made our interest in Nicklaus even more heightened; it seemed magical with its dark grey fairways, white-sanded bunkers and billiard-table-top smooth, light grey greens. We had to imagine the glorious shades of green on the black and white screen. At least golf didn't create the headache that *Pot Black* gave me when trying to distinguish between the white and the pink or the brown and the blue — unless Ted Lowe was commentating and catered for us black and white telly plebs. It would be another five years before I witnessed the splendour of colour on the screen!

Most of the potholes in the road were small, anything from three inches to ten inches in diameter — perfect to knock a tennis ball into. So we scoured the new golf course and marked each hole in the tarmac with a number in chalk. There were only fifteen suitable holes so we agreed to play holes one to three twice in the round. We made chalk circles to indicate where the tennis ball should be placed to tee off. We only had one cricket bat so we decided to use our Woolworths tennis racquets as golf clubs — fussing around with only one bat would have spoiled the fun of it all. I always find it amazing how you can learn the rules of a sport just by watching it on the telly — yet never actually playing it. Golf, tennis, snooker, show jumping and rugby league were classic examples. I liked the way golf was scored on par, so me and Paul adopted the same for our course. We wanted to give holes a mixture of par scores so we made sure the tee circle varied in distance from its corresponding hole. That allowed us to have three par fives, five par fours and the rest par threes. Playing the first three holes twice gave us a course par score of sixty-five. The cardboard box that the Sugar Puffs came in (they were an unusual treat from the standard and cheaper cornflakes) gave us our scorecard. We loved to commentate too, to give a real-time feel to our competition. It was tricky to get the accuracy at first but we both found our way by the time we started the second round of four. By the time we started the fourth round, I was seventeen under par and Paul was sixteen under par. Some of our mates came out to watch and I felt like a real celebrity. I was Arnold Palmer and Paul was Lee Trevino — we agreed that neither of us could be the great Jack Nicklaus.

Then BANG! A car bomb explosion in the vicinity of Carlisle Road. No others followed but the helicopters appeared from the barracks, the ambulances and RUC jeeps played their siren symphonies and everyone came out of their houses to see what was happening. Our course was overrun with spectators of a non-sporty kind and the true spectators disappeared over the Tins to get a better view of the black smoke that rose into the now-greying sky. Our Four Streets Open golf competition was ruined. We knew we'd have to wait for a bit till everything settled down and for our course to be vacated once again — it took about an hour. The usual guessing of exactly where the bomb had targeted and the anticipation of the next car bomb going off was followed by more general street gossip about neighbours or near neighbours; who had been arrested or been in a fight or gone off to borstal. After what seemed an eternity, we could restart the golf, as the most gossipy women in the Four Streets retreated to their shiny front doorsteps, arms duly folded across their floral pinnies. We did a quick check of the course to ensure that it was still fit for purpose and got to the first tee at the bottom of York Street in front of the small row of three houses that ran parallel to the road and at a right angle to the main street. It was Paul's turn to tee off, but no sooner had he practised his tennis racquet swing, we felt a few very heavy drops of rain on our heads. The clouds that had been building up their rain over our heads during the bomb interruption let fall their cargo. It took seconds before there was a thunder plump — extremely heavy rain that might accompany thunder, but without the thunder. As we ran for the house, I could see the chalk numbers and chalk circles being washed away. I knew Derry rain and its behaviour as it swept across from the west and the hills of Donegal. I knew then too, that we wouldn't be able to play after the rain had stopped. Game over.

Normally I would have claimed a victory over my greatest adversary, but I was so gutted that, once again, the rain and a bomb robbed us of camaraderie, competition and choice. Life was sure a roller coaster of peaks and troughs! We all know that a first experience cannot not be replicated or replayed or reincarnated. The magical and special feeling that can come from such an experience, like our first game of golf, is lost as soon as it's over. We often repeat a positive first experience, but we know that, despite the pleasure and enjoyment gained, it's never the same — it's never the same feeling. Luckily, me and Paul would forever create some new game, some new sport and conjure up a new kind of magical experience — to try and escape the bombs and the rain.

I guess all attempts to escape the bombs and the rain were, in essence, pretty futile. Me, Paul, everyone around us got accustomed to the Troubles and all its parts, but it didn't stop us from living our lives. Yes, we had to adapt as populations in any war-torn country adapts to the death and destruction around them. Even when Ma dragged me and Paul out of Littlewoods after the RUC had come in to evacuate the store, owing to a bomb warning a hundred yards away, I just thought, oh here we go again. In fact, the bomb went off in the carpet shop just as we got outside. The incredulity of the noise was only outdone by the amount of bellowing black smoke that shot out through broken glass. Ma was terrified whilst me and Paul wanted to look on as we were fascinated — for once I could understand Da's fascination of seeing an event live and not on the telly. I guess Ma felt responsible for our safety and I know it was some months before she ventured over to the Strand Road to shop again.

Those looking in to the Troubles from the outside, usually via their television screens, would only see the snapshot of life and culture that the person behind the camera chose to portray. You had to live in it and experience it, to understand it. Even then, there was too much to try and understand. How could I understand the killings, the bombings, the bigotry, the prejudice, the fear, when no one really took pains to educate me? Maybe this was down to me own inadequacy and lack of education. Ma, Da, me relatives, me neighbours, me teachers, me minister, saw the world through their own individual lenses. Some lenses were portrait, some landscape, some wide-angle, but they still contained a bias, a narrow view — maybe this is always the way? So, confusion and insubstantial doctrine ruled. Therefore, it was both useful and educational to have the 'English' families visit for six weeks for a few summers.

Susan Boyd and Janine Smith were two women who had spent their childhood and youth living in Alfred Street, but had taken the well-trodden journey by Irish folk to mainland Britain (always referred to as England) for jobs. They got married and had families. In the summer they returned for the six weeks of the

English schools' summer holidays to stay with their mothers (fathers had passed away) along with their own children. This brought kids with alien accents and alien clothes to me own street. It also brought kids with questions — lots of questions. Questions about why we lived the way we did, why we spoke the way we did, why we murdered each other, why we bombed and rioted, and what was the difference between Protestants and Catholics when we were all Christians. I found the English perspectives stimulating as it related to me own questions. I was glad to have 'alien' buddies who thought like me, yet they felt confident to voice their thoughts in contrast to me who just felt small, insignificant and troublesome and who was too frightened to speak out or speak up.

After the initial ritual of embarrassment and awkwardness when the English first arrived, it didn't take long till they became part of our friendship group and of all the activities that we immersed ourselves in during the long summer off school. Children just don't have the same hang-ups as adults when integrating with strangers. We taught them our games and they taught us theirs, but it was the teaching of how to kiss a girl properly and to have some inner feelings for a girl that stands out in me memory.

Brigid Evans was the daughter of Susan Boyd (now Susan Evans through marriage) and was a year older than me. Her granny lived only three doors up from me own house, but on the opposite side of the street. I was ten and had been doing a paper round, delivering the Tele (*Belfast Telegraph*) since I was eight; I delivered it daily to her granny's house. By the time I'd get to her granny's house, I was knackered from the long walk around Ebrington Terrace, May Street, Bond's Street, Clondermot Road, Dungiven Court, Dungiven Road and Clooney Terrace.

I'd start outside the old people's home on Limavady Road — that's where the bales of Teles were dropped off and where I met up with Isaac, the Tele man. No one knew Isaac's surname but everyone knew him as he'd been the Tele man for decades. He always wore an old black suit, a shirt that had long since lost its whiteness, and a worn-out pair of grey fingerless gloves. His permanent purple face (like that of an alcoholic's, though he was teetotal) glowed brightly regardless of the season. He only wore an old dirty-brown gabardine if it was lashing it down before he left his house, but many a time he would then get soaked when the rain came *after* he'd left. He could easily have popped back to get it, but never did. I believe he was the only Irishman or Irishwoman I knew who didn't prepare for the rain!

I'd be at the Tele rendezvous at ten past five every day. I was always on time as I hated being late for anything. Punctuality was made easier as I only lived a two-minute sprint away. Isaac would always already be there with the bales of Teles; about a hundred broadsheet-size papers per bale. Each bale was very tightly tied up with cord in a criss-cross pattern to allow for easy lifting and chucking on to a van or out of a van. Isaac would greet me with his customary monosyllabic "Right" and I would respond with a nod of the head. He was not a conversationalist so if the paper van was late, there would be awkward silences between us, peppered thankfully by someone passing by who would have a quick chat with him about how he was, the weather, the papers being late, the news, the horses (he frequented the bookies that was twenty yards away from his house). He could chat as long as the other person drove the conversation.

I'd stand still with me arms outstretched as he tied the bale cord around me waist and then with a long piece hanging from me left side, he'd create a loop for me hand to slip through. I'd watch him count fifty-six Teles and then place them over the long hanging piece of cord, the middle fold resting on it. I'd then use me hip and arm to balance the papers, helped by their weight. I built up a stamina and a strength over the first few months of delivering the papers, but the first week nearly killed me — the weight was horrendous whilst the balancing act left me with pains all up me left arm, left side and left wrist! There was one crucial consolation — the weight got lighter with the more I delivered or sold. Forty-six of the Teles were for house deliveries whilst the other ten were for cash-buying. There would be the odd person who'd stop me for a paper and I would get paid, often with a tip. During the round I'd pop into three bars, one on Clondermot Road and two on Dungiven Road. This was me first taste of smoke-filled, beer-smelling, noisy bars. I hated walking into the crowds of working men, or dole men who were either drunk or well on their way to being drunk. Drinking beer in a bar was the only thing that united Catholics and Protestants (to some degree) other than Manchester United. Religion and all its symbolism and hatred-fuelled facets seemed to be left to slumber outside each bar, but was duly awakened once a staggering drunk ventured back into the jungle street. Fights rarely took place inside a bar; it was always outside of it. Once I was inside one of the bars and shouted "Tele" a few times, there would always be a few people who would send a hand into a pocket for the change to buy one off me. More often than not, I wouldn't have to use the kitty of change that Isaac had given me for giving someone their change. I'd be waved away with a hand or a brusque "Keep the change, wee lad". Me heart would leap every time I had cash that was me own and I would feel the wave of excitement from head to toe, yet not show it till I was on me own. A quick shake of me fist to celebrate, just as I would when scoring a goal, was me own way of celebrating and for allowing me body to calm down with the cathartic release it brought.

The monetary rewards of going into the bars made the torture of it all worthwhile. Further monetary gain was to be had at Christmas when I'd be handed a handsome tip from nearly all the houses I delivered to.

I would have to knock on each door to hand-deliver the Tele instead of just dropping it through the letter box. I hated when someone wasn't in, though there were a few kind souls who would go out of their way at some later point in time, to hand me a tip. Only a couple of miserly, grumpy folk didn't give any sort of tip — they were the ones that I'd save the wettest paper for — the one on the outside of the batch that was least sheltered by me arm and me body.

Of course, the paper round had its pitfalls too. There was the dark nights, the adverse weather and the venturing into Clooney Courts. The street lighting that came on during the winter months was as dim as the light that the twenty-five-watt bulbs gave out in our bedrooms — only the main roads had any light that made me feel at ease. The streets made me feel much more on edge, especially when I had some change rattling around in me pocket. I would have been defenceless to anyone bigger than me. The fact that people didn't venture out in the dark and the rain if they could help it, or were indoors in the warmth of their houses having their tea, meant that I'd often be walking the streets on me own. Luckily, I hadn't been subject to the slasher movies that appeared in our living rooms in the late seventies and the following decades. So me imagination was only triggered by the likes of the Cybermen. It was more of the anxious, body fear that was always there, more than the fear of something actually happening to me. The darkness, the blackness was all-consuming. There was no lighting at all along on the road at the bottom of the Four Streets. There was the crossing of the black lanes at the top of each street to navigate, there was dark and urine-smelling staircases at the flats of Clooney Court, and then there was the dark, creepy, narrow staircases on Clooney Terrace that led down to the dark and dingy basement flats. Once I had been given a few warning punches and kicks from the Catholic boys at Clooney Court (I wasn't seen as a major threat), the staircases weren't too scary. It was more the darkness, the smell and the icy coldness that instilled the fear in me. The basement flats on Clooney Terrace were a different experience altogether.

By the time I got to Clooney Terrace, rush hour traffic had passed and the street became very still and quiet. It was a one-way street and most traffic that was headed towards Duke Street or the bridge went down Bond's Hill, so cars would only pass me sporadically. Two of me paper drop-offs were basement flats, or hovels as I'd call them. One was to a man in his fifties and one was to a woman in her seventies — they both seemed to live alone. They both frightened the living daylights out of me if they appeared when I was delivering the Tele, or if I had the courage to knock for me Christmas tip. I'm not sure who scared me the most, the man who fitted the horrible stereotype of a child molester with his sickly-coloured skin and filthy clothes, or the woman with her bony frame, long scraggy grey hair and gapped teeth. They, and their

265

flats, stank of mould, fried food and of the smell of Uncle Billy's slops that were fed to the pig. The stone staircase that led to each basement was often littered with rubbish, old Teles, bits of food left for the cats, moss and any other weed that thrived on damp conditions. Of course, there would be slugs, snails, spiders and wood lice to navigate. When I'd reach the bottom, I felt like I was in a First World War trench at night, with the occasional rat to keep me company (I saw many a rat too). I'd look up to see a darkness surrounding me with only the faintest of light that stretched from the nearest lamp post. Me body was always in a state of tension and I would clench the already-rolled-up Tele in me right hand, ready to quickly push through the letter box. I couldn't move quickly for fear of falling or slipping. Even in the summer months, the steps barely dried out, whilst the outstretched arms of the weeds would be ready to grab me and swallow me up. I couldn't picture living in one of those basements, with no real natural light getting in, in any season. I often wondered how the old man and old woman ended up living in them and what kind of life they had and had had. I don't recall ever seeing them out and about beyond their caves — a forgotten element of society that exists everywhere in the world. By the time I was done with Clooney Terrace, me last furlong was the Four Streets.

It was one early July evening, after I'd dropped off the Tele to me own house and to Mrs Campbell's next door, that I started to cross the street to old Mrs Boyd's house. I hadn't seen the English contingent arrive that day and was met with Brigid at the door. She and her brothers and sisters had been over from London the last two years and we played together and had a laugh, but this time she looked different — there was something about her that I liked. She gave me a big smile which sent me into a state of redness.

"Hello, Sidney," she beamed. "We got here earlier today."

"Ah, right," I blurted beneath the redness.

"Still doing that paper round I see." Her voice was confident.

"I might as well. There's a bit of money for me in it."

"Well, it's good to see you. Perhaps we'll play later, yeah?"

"Sure, that'd be great."

I don't know how I managed to smile back at her, but I did. Then out came her brothers and sisters to see who Brigid had been talking to. I then quickly waved and hurried up to the next house that ached for the latest news in the Tele. Me face was aching too, to lose its heat. By the time I got to Isaac's Tele HQ and waited to give him the money for the ten Teles I'd sold, me face had restored its natural colour. But feelings inside of me hadn't reached a similar state of equilibrium. It was something to do with Brigid, but I didn't know what.

Playing games with me mates and with the English

happened as it had done the previous two years. Brigid was her usual self, bubbly and confident. She didn't give me that same smile, as she'd done on the first day she'd arrived but we got on well. It was pretty typical of all of us in the Four Streets to get on with each other, regardless of religious persuasion, and the same was true of the English kids when they arrived. Brigid was no different towards me than the other boys, but I was aware that a closeness of some kind was present. We played our usual games with a ball, with a skipping rope, with marbles. Team competitions were created too, but it wasn't until we played Touch that the kiss happened.

In Touch we would divide into about four groups of three or four. The group who was 'on it' had to wait in someone's porch or front door and count to one hundred to give the others the chance to escape and hide. The 'on it' team had to physically touch the others, who then became part of the 'on it' team — and so on till one person was left the winner. The last team to be 'on it' was mine — me, Brian and Helen. I was quick, nimble on me feet and confident at knowing the 'good' spots to hide. So I decided I'd first search over the Tins, whilst the other two chose a street to go up. I climbed to the Tins via the easiest spot — through a splintered sleeper that allowed me to keep low as I entered the waste ground. When playing commandos, I'd proudly climb over a tall sleeper to show off me skills, but this was a time to be more subtle about me entrance. I crept around the Tins, bent forwards so as not to be seen and give meself away, and pausing every now and again to take stock of the Tins and do a slow three-hundred-and-sixty-degree reconnaissance in order to detect any movement. The grass and weeds had grown tall so there was a good screen for me too.

Chuck, chuck, chuck, chuck, chuck, chuck, chuck. There's the copter off again I thought. I hadn't heard a bomb go off so it must be a shooting somewhere — guns or rifles going off were more difficult to hear unless they were near the river. I switched into commando mode and jumped into the nearest crater — one of many in the Tins. I had nothing to be scared of but I liked to show off me agility even if no one else was watching. To me surprise I landed right next to Brigid. She gave a tiny scream as I landed but she was already in a state of shock with the copter flying overhead. She clearly wasn't used to this sound back in London. I touched her arm as we were still playing Touch — a game was a game! She immediately put her arms around me — I could feel her trembling. Normally I would have made a joke of her being scared, but her pale face, shaking body and tight clenching of me own body made me decide that this wasn't the right time for a wise craic.

Neither of us spoke for the next five minutes. I was in an unusual place; I hadn't been this close to a girl before and certainly not for this length of time. I could feel her warm, soft body against mine. When Brigid eventually raised her head from me chest, she looked at me and kissed me slowly on the lips. There was no red face from me this time; I wasn't embarrassed and it all felt right. She pulled back and rested her head on the grass. There were still no words uttered as I leaned over her and kissed her. The soft, wet and tender lips were a pure joy to me. I'd quickly kissed the odd girl at school in the past, but this was different; this was lovely. We kissed and kissed and kissed some more. The only words we shared after we had lain for at least five minutes was that we thought the other was a good kisser. Voices of others brought us out from the crater and we continued with the game as if nothing had happened, but we knew something had. From that day on till the end of Brigid's stay, we smiled at each other a lot and met up in secret a few times for the kissing. The others knew that we fancied each other and did a bit of teasing, but we were only young. There was no sense of being in love, there was no sexual arousal, there was no feeling of wild passion — all that was to come once puberty kicked in a few years later. There was something extremely innocent about what we had, something simple, something pure, something natural. The last time I would see Brigid was her waving from her granny's doorstep the night before she was due to leave early the next morning. Her granny died the following spring and her mother and father came for the funeral, but neither Brigid nor her siblings came for that event. I never saw her again. Yet another first experience that would never be recaptured. Future relationships with girls and women would prove much more complex, much more intense and much more soul-wrenching! How we all hark back to such simplicity.

Further simplicity and innocence were present (initially) a summer earlier when me and Paul got a band going, just like the marching bands we'd see on the streets on the 12th July and 12th August. The flutes, the accordions and the drums were part of me 'Orange' culture, though I knew nothing about Irish history in general. The symbolism of the bands and lodges and the impact on me Catholic neighbours of this culture was lost on me. It was lost on me for many years during the Troubles. Later in me teens and a chance listening to Irish folk music, and an even later further education would bring me a different psyche and a different culture.

All me mates, regardless of religious persuasion, joined up with us to create a flute band on a number of occasions. The Tins provided all the materials we needed — clearly an early form of recycling! There were old, rusty milk tins that were the perfect size for drums — about twelve inches in diameter and about two feet deep. I never knew where these came from, but like lots of the rubbish that was dumped over the Tins, it didn't just come from households but from small local shops too. Some of the big boys would boast about getting paid to dump stuff from the shop owners once it got dark. So I assume that's where the milk tins came from. There was an endless supply of string or cord —

of different strengths and of different colours, but that didn't matter. As long as we could thread a piece through the holes, we'd make in the milk tins and they were long enough to reach around the drummer's neck, then that would suffice. There was also an endless supply of wood to provide us with flutes. There were branches off trees, legs off chairs, broken staffs off brushes and spindles off bannisters. All of these could be cut to a suitable length and have imitation holes carved out by a screwdriver. The stick for the drum major was purely a matter of using the metal tubular spindle of a bed frame that still had the brass knob attached. The competition was rife to produce the best drum, the best flute and the best mace — there were hours of preparation. None of us saw the significance of any of me Catholic mates participating in what was part of a Protestant culture. They would have watched the parades just like me and Paul did, and although they might not have learnt the songs that accompanied some of the tunes, they knew the tunes. I knew some words but didn't have any idea what they meant or stood for — I guess I wasn't alone.

When we'd finished our carpentry, metalwork and furniture-making, we'd decide who was playing what role, what instrument. Some of us would have to agree to take turns at playing the drums as this was perceived as the most treasured role. Making the most noise probably had some influence in this craving!

Our inaugural march was a great success. We

whistled 'Derry's Walls' and 'The Sash' and it brought out loads of people from their homes with smiles on their faces — a few people even clapped. Up and down the Four Streets we marched. I was the drum major on this first march and practised the art of starting us all off with a 'by the left, quick march' and counting down from four to one to start the whistling. I hadn't practised spinning the mace like I'd seen others do in marches so I just moved it back and fore from me chest to an arm's length in front of me. But I had learned that if I blew on me thumb for a bit, it loosened the muscles around me mouth and this produced a much stronger whistle. Me and Paul had practised this many times to create a powerful shrill. So I told the others about it. Jimmy and Johnny wouldn't do it as they said it was a bit like sucking your thumb, whilst Mary and Lizzy couldn't whistle for their supper, so no amount of blowing on their thumb mattered. They still tried, and made some kind of noise. Being drum major also meant that I had the authority to bring a tune to an end by raising me mace. I never thought I'd feel at ease being the forefront of attention. Neither did I know that, in me late teens, I'd be the temporary drum major for Culmore Pipe Band! On the second march we held, we decided to hum the tunes so that everyone could fully participate.

However, by the time we held our third march at the end of August 1971, the feeling in the Four Streets mirrored that of Northern Ireland in general. More killings, bombings and deaths led to greater community divisions and inter-religious tensions. Tolerance of difference became less too. A change firstly became evident when Jimmy, Sean and Gerry would show off their bruises having been hit by rubber bullets when rioting on the Bogside. They would walk over the town with school mates to join in the battles with the police. It was all a bit of fun to them, to chuck bricks, stones and anything else they could get their hands on, at the RUC. They hated them and had heard too many stories of Catholics being mistreated by them and the B Specials. It was their way of fighting back and making a stance against unfair brutality. I'd see images on the telly of rioting and always saw the rioters in the wrong and the police in the right. The more I listened to their stories, the more I became confused — the police were about establishing law and order, weren't they, just like a US Marshall in a western when he jailed any outlaw? How could a mob of stone-throwers be right, have a cause to fight like this for? I had a lot to learn about politics, history, religious bias and bigotry.

These boys had no desire to be part of our band that represented a culture that they now rejected. Other Catholic mates followed out of loyalty to them and a perceived allegiance, so our numbers were severely depleted. However, it soon became clear as seven of us marched up Florence Street, that the Catholic boys' stance was not an isolated one. For the first time, some Catholic neighbours came out and gave us some verbals to stop, which brought reprisals from Protestant neighbours. Everything suddenly felt wrong and tense and the innocence turned sour, so we stopped. We threw our instruments back over the Tins from where we'd found them, never to be used again. I felt a darkness and tension that I hadn't experienced before in the Four Streets. By the time I headed off to Faughan Valley Secondary Modern in September 1973, the Troubles had taken a severe grip on everyone, the telly, the radio, adult conversations, mates and now ex-mates. Faughan Valley only served to heighten this darkness as I came into contact with many others who heralded from miles beyond the Four Streets and the Waterside.

The eleven-plus exam was often the fork in the roadway that potentially mapped out the rest of your life. It either sent you on to the path that led to a grammar school education, possibly university and a more affluent life, or the path that led to a secondary education, where formal education ended and a life of lower-paid work and financial struggle or even to a life on the dole beckoned. Me and Paul passed the eleven-plus exam, much to the utter shock from Ma and Da and me three older sisters who had passed it and gone to the grammar school, Londonderry High School. We came down for breakfast one Saturday morning in June 1973 and found Ma holding a letter that told her we had passed. We both felt great, purely on the basis that we had achieved something that was deemed by all parents as the epitome of educational success and something that was hard to attain. We were also a bit deflated as

Ma and Da didn't really congratulate us and didn't seem too thrilled by our success. We soon found out why. Neither me nor Paul had thought about going to the grammar school, Foyle College, as the boys who had hoped to go there heralded from the more affluent and snobby areas such as Hinton Park and Caw Park. We got on with them but there were clear differences between us and them. Saying that, there were also clear differences between us and many of the boys who were destined to a secondary education. What school should we go to? We talked to each other about the grammar boys and about the fact they didn't play our beloved football there, and instead played something called rugby. I had no idea what rugby was, yet lived and breathed for football. Ma tried to get our true feelings out of us about what school we wanted to go to in order not to hurt us with their views. For a few days, I could hear Ma and Da whispering about the school situation — their voices were serious. Eventually, they sat me and Paul down to tell us that we were not going to go to Foyle College as they couldn't afford to send us there on top of already subsidising Irene, Hazel and Val to go to their grammar school. The decision was not ours. I felt robbed of being the one to make the choice and it felt unfair too that three sisters could carry on their eleven-plus success, but we couldn't. I didn't know much about education and what it can do for you in later years, but having gone to Faughan Valley, I know too well about the struggle that a poor education can have on your future working life.

The first day at Faughan Valley Secondary Modern didn't particularly start well. We newbies started for a half a day before the rest of the school and were hoarded into the assembly hall to be divided into our classes. Ebrington Primary had an assembly hall but this one looked huge and much more foreboding. Name by name was called out but neither me own name nor Paul's name was called out — along with a handful of others. Up until a couple of weeks before school started, me and Paul were destined for Clondermot Secondary School, situated on the edge of the council estate, Irish Street. The school was only a hundred and fifty yards away from Gobnascale, the Catholic area that the IRA snipers fired from when shooting at security forces on Craigavon Bridge. I knew some of the 'rough' boys who went there and coupled by its proximity to Gobnascale, the prospect of going there didn't exactly leave me with a bag of excitement. Robin and Mina had both gone to Clondermot but that was before the Troubles had started. Ma and Da had their reservations (even before a high dividing fence was erected, to separate the two areas) and at the eleventh hour arranged a meeting with the head of Faughan Valley. They were impressed by his rhetoric and on that basis, switched schools for me and Paul. However, the administration of the switch hadn't been completed, so our names were called out for the identical assembly hall gathering at Clondermot instead. The head of first form then took me and Paul to his office and allocated us to our form class — we were given different classes! We never had imagined that we wouldn't be together as we'd been in the same class since nursery and all through primary school. Suddenly, the 'big' school felt even more intimidating and daunting. By the time I was taken to the form classroom (one of about twelve portakabins as the school had expanded its intake due to the boom in the birth rate for my year), Mrs Burns had just started the roll call. I felt me face burn as I arrived late and to be stared at by the rest of the class — I so hated being the centre of attention unless it was on me own terms as captain of the football team or commando squadron leader with me mates. After the spotlight was off me, I had a good look at the others in class. I recognised eight or nine faces from primary school, Sunday school or football matches, and nodded at them, but the rest were completely alien to me.

I wasn't long at the school before I learned where the diverse population of the school came from. There were those like me from the Waterside area — the working-class areas of the Four Streets, Bond's Street, Lincoln Courts, Irish Street, Nelson Drive and the posher residential area of Woodburn, that I had never even walked through. Woodburn houses looked so neat with their red brick houses and bungalows and thick, brown-tiled roofs. I'd pass this area on the bus — it was in stark contrast to the Four Streets. Me familiar high, glassed-topped walls that housed concrete backyards were replaced by low walls at the front, that housed a pretty garden and a slightly higher wall that housed a huge back garden. Little did I know that six months later I would find out exactly what it was like to live there! So, apart from the Waterside crowd at Faughan Valley, who made up about a third of the pupil population, the others came from far-outreaching places I had never heard of. There were the locals from Drumahoe, those from the huge executive housing estates of Maydown and Strathfoyle to the north of Derry, those from the huge executive housing estate of Newbuildings to the south of Derry, and then there were the country folk who commuted from the farming places of Goshedan, Killaloo and Claudy, and everywhere in between.

What this mix of population had in common was a strong Protestant and Loyalist mentality — more extreme than I had ever experienced. In the Four Streets I was aware of difference in terms of religion and religious background, but there was a tolerance, although slowly evaporating, that allowed me to have connections and friendships with Catholics. This 'new' populace had no room for difference or indeed for Catholics. The nearest I got to this mindset was from those I knew in the Waterside executive housing estate of Irish Street, where the kerbs were painted red, white and blue and union jacks and the 'red hand of Ulster' flags flew from every other telegraph pole. Yet, some of the boys there mixed with Catholic boys on the football field and even on the same team at times. The boys from the 'foreign' fields to me would be in a band, accordion or flute, as a way of maintaining Protestant/Ulster culture and heritage. They would frequently criticise Catholics as being 'all IRA', refer to them as 'Taigs' and 'Fenians' at every opportunity (terms I was aware of but not heard in constant usage), state they were 'British' and not Irish like them, and brag about giving any of them a kicking when the opportunity arose. All of a sudden, me and Paul found ourselves in the middle, on the fence, having what's best described as a liberal or moderate way of thinking. I knew I wasn't the only one thinking like this but it was clear that we all toed the line so as not to be totally alienated from the 'Orange' majority. So when a drummer from one of the bands started drumming with his pencils in class (when the teacher was a weak one), it was never long before he was joined by more drummers and then flute players, whistling the 'Sash'. Of course, I'd fit in and join in, but always felt uncomfortable about such a strong display of Protestantism. I also felt uncomfortable for the poor teacher who clearly had not gained any respect from these pupils. Miss Campbell the geography teacher, Mr McNeil the religious education teacher and Mrs Carmichael the French teacher were the ones whose classes became the 12th of July parade on a regular basis. I didn't like any of these subjects, but I knew it was wrong to take over the class in the way these Loyalist-minded pupils did. I guess the teachers felt frightened to challenge this show of force too, and didn't even report it to the head. I would remind meself of Ma and Da being easily taken in by the head's rhetoric which led to the switching of schools for me and Paul. However, they would have been seemingly intimidated by a man who was formally educated in a way they were not and whose use of vocabulary and powers of persuasion were likely to outdo their own.

I never told Ma and Da about these band situations at school, just like I never told them much at all about school (I think all of you can relate to that?). They found out over time what Faughan Valley was like as a school and regretted sending me and Paul there at the last minute. What was then very difficult to do as a consequence of this new 'schooling', was to meet up with me Catholic friends when I got home from school and pretend that nothing had changed — but it had. They were obviously experiencing a similar kind of indoctrination in their own schools. So, the religious divide that was as wide as a trickling brook when we first left primary school, soon became as wide, as murky and as tempestuous as the River Foyle itself! Sadly, what was happening in me own world was a clear reflection of what was happening in the world of the Troubles around me; division quickly became opposition, which quickly became hatred, which quickly became an excuse to kill and murder. I felt trapped somewhere in the middle of all this polarisation. A mere consolation was that I wasn't alone; there were plenty of other 'middle-of-the-roaders'. Unfortunately, our voices were never spoken or heard; fear of reprisals, retaliation or retribution for not being so-called partisan to the religious side that we were born into put paid to that. Going along with the 'majority' was what me and everyone else did — if only in terms of not opposing them!

The religious divide that was taking shape in the Four Streets was tangible and scary. I didn't fear the Catholic boys that I had grown up with — a sense of a shared history and innate loyalty allowed for tolerance between us. However, the Protestant boys they didn't know, or their Catholic friends who didn't know me, didn't allow for any sentimentality. If I bumped into other Catholic boys who didn't know me, I would be questioned and assessed on me loyalty to the 'Orange' cause and me associations with Loyalist bands. I'd also be checked out if I was on their wanted list of boys who had been responsible for beating up any of their mates. I never got beaten up but got the odd kick and punch as a warning. What was harder to stomach was seeing an old Catholic mate being picked on or slapped about by Protestant boys who didn't see them as an old mate — but purely as the enemy. Hearing boys at school bragging about beating up Catholic boys turned me stomach — I hated violence. Another challenge was pretending to support such bragging and seem enthusiastically interested — it takes an extremely strong voice to speak against a strong majority! Thankfully, me 'voice' eventually came, albeit years later.

This school confliction was going to be with me for five years, but the tension in the Four Streets was going to be less of a sentence — I was going to escape it. Just before Christmas arrived in 1973, Ma and Da suddenly announced that we were going to move house — we were going to Lisnagelvin — an extension of Woodburn! They said that the council were definitely going to build a dual carriageway and offered residents who lived in the bottom half of the Four Streets a good deal to buy their houses. Even though this wasn't going to happen for eighteen to twenty-four months, Ma and Da didn't want to hang around and perhaps be offered less at some point in the future, so they decided they'd sell up. They were likely too, to be more aware of the tensions building amongst those in the Four Streets, and that the more affluent area of Lisnagelvin would house less tension.

Me initial thoughts were negative ones. What was Lisnagelvin like? Woodburn looked posh from the bus. What kind of people lived there? What about me mates in the Four Streets? I didn't know this place whereas I knew the Four Streets so well I could walk around blindfold. What about the football matches over the Tins or on the bottom road? What about me paper round — Lisnagelvin seemed miles away? Would me and Paul have our own bedroom as we now had in Alfred Street? I kept all these questions to meself — what was the point in asking Ma or Da? They'd only tell me not to ask questions. There was no point in asking me sisters either; they'd just laugh. There was no point in asking Paul; he was no wiser than me. In fact, Paul did his usual thing of not wanting to talk about it and buried his head in a book.

It was in the January when Ma and Da told us all that they had the keys and that we could go and visit the new house. They had obviously been planning the move for months without telling us. When did parents start talking to their kids about such traumatic events to help them re-adjust to the change that lay ahead? We were told in December and the plan was to move the following March. So that left four months to leave everything I knew for somewhere that I didn't know from Eden. This was the second time I felt in a kind of limbo, a kind of void, a kind of lost — the last time was when baby sister Isobel arrived in Ma's arms almost six years before.

# Chapter 12
## Isobel, the Last Born

Either I hadn't been told or didn't pay any attention, but Ma was obviously pregnant and carrying Isobel for nine months, and I hadn't noticed. The near-six-year gap told its own story about family planning — all the rest of us were born between eighteen months and three years apart. Me and Paul were playing a game of blow football in the kitchen. Normally we'd play that in the sitting room, but Ma and Da were out 'somewhere' and me sisters were in there, so the kitchen was all ours which didn't happen very often. The next minute, there was a great commotion in the hallway and Ma appeared with this baby in a basket telling us that here was our baby sister. I could see how the birth of baby Jesus was easily believed as a miracle — no baby one minute, and a baby the next! Me and Paul weren't interested in this new baby, unlike me sisters who had a real live baby doll to feed, change and coo over. We quickly took a look at her. She was sleeping, so headed off to continue our blow football game in the now-vacated sitting room.

I guess this was how our relationship with Isobel was founded; she was virtually six years younger, only a little baby, and a girl at that. Of course, me and Paul had each other; we had our games, our battles, our space and didn't want an invader around. Time would grant me permission to take on the typical older brother role of protecting me baby sister, but this was still a number of years away. Right now, I wasn't interested.

Isobel, like the rest of us, had her moments of escape from threatening situations — one was when a baby and the other was in the summer before we moved house. The baby escape was more one of luck than anything else.

St Columb's Park was a ten-minute walk away from our house and Val, Hazel and Irene decided they'd take Isobel for a walk in her pram — it was her maiden voyage beyond the Four Streets and the first time that Ma trusted me sisters with the responsibility for a six-month-old away from the safety of her bosom. It was in July during the long school holidays and on a sunny day after days of torrential rain that swept in from the Atlantic and over the Donegal hills. Everyone had felt cooped up in the house and tensions were beginning to emerge as tolerance and patience levels rapidly dropped. Mina and Robin had full-time jobs; Mina in a typing pool and Robin fixing television aerials to people's chimneys. Da was obviously at work too, but that left five of us, Ma, and screaming, crying baby Isobel. So when the sun finally came out and gave us a bit of summer warmth of twenty degrees Celsius (that was a heatwave in Derry), me sisters jumped at the chance to take Isobel out in her new pram. The pram that me and Paul had had long been sold on as Ma and Da had probably thought that the family was big enough and there wouldn't be use of it again. I wondered what it was like having a big-wheeled pram all to yourself — the space to move around and the comfort of not being kicked or squashed by a bigger twin. Ma set Isobel up in the pram with the usual hand-knitted pink cardigan; this one was one of Aunt Jean's products and was complete with ribbon to tie a bow at the top. There was no bonnet or mittens this time. Ma had long gone past the overprotectiveness that new mothers can have and who can smother their baby with clothes and blankets regardless of the weather and season. After all, she'd had seven others prior to Isobel and had no time for impracticalities, fussing or spending time overdoing motherhood. Irene, Hazel and Val had asked if they could take her to St Columb's Park which was bold of them at the time. Ma didn't hesitate to say yes as she was in bad need of some space and to get her head shired (Derry for head cleared) after days of cabin fever induced by the wetness that had engulfed the Four Streets. Me and Paul had first thought of not going with them but the temptation of going to the play park with the 'Banana' slide, the massive roundabout and the swings was too good to miss.

So we set off after dinner in the early afternoon, me sisters on the pavement with the pram and me and Paul on the road passing our football back and fore. As if by some sixth sense that told mothers and girls that a pram was in the street, out they all came to see our procession. It seemed to take ages to get to the top of the street as they all wanted a glimpse, a stare, a peek at Isobel. There was one pair of folded arms, one head scarf and one pinny after another. It was going to take more than ten minutes to get to the park this time. Me sisters took great pride at showing off the latest addition to the Kennedy stock, but me and Paul were frustrated. Even the walk along Melrose Terrace which led to the busy Limavady Road and that took us to our beloved park seemed to have more pedestrians than normal. Of course, there were those who knew us as a family and repeated the behaviour that had taken place on our street. Me and Paul didn't even have the luxury of kicking the ball about as we were next to the main road — even bouncing it on the pavement would have been a sin and been reported back to Ma, and then later to Da.

Going through the gates of the park was a great feeling, all inhibitions gone. I could only be there if someone else took me there and it was a couple of years before I felt brave enough to sneak there with me mates. The new leisure centre was starting to be built near the entrance to the park and there were diggers, wheelbarrows, steel girders, noise and mud everywhere. The Waterside never had a leisure centre before so this created its own sense of excitement. Luckily, the main path down to the play park was still intact. I could smell the trees, the stream, the dampness of the rain drying as it rose into the air in a mild mist. There wasn't the fusty, stale smell that resided over the Tins and that seemed to stay trapped within its boundaries. Here, was energy, life, growth and an unrestricted freedom. Unfortunately, me sisters didn't want to take the direct route to the park and veered off up the narrower path that rose up away from the stream some twenty-five feet and went in a straight line along the three football pitches. It would eventually taper down to the play park at the end but it would be an unwanted detour. Me and Paul moaned to them but they were as formidable as Macbeth's witches when they got together and weren't having any of it. It was their walk, and we had purely thumbed a lift so had no say in the direction we headed. Out of a meagre form of resistance, we were allowed to stay on the main path but within clear view of the sisters with the pram up on the steep bank. It felt like they were the Apache or the Zulu, outnumbering us two to one and who had all the ammunition and know-how to keep us right where they wanted to! At least we could knock our football about. Then I became aware that me sisters had lagged behind a bit and were talking to some boys. I could tell that Hazel and Val knew them by the silly giggling at anything they said. I didn't recognise them so guessed they were grammar school boys. Hazel shouted for us to climb up the banking as they were going to get some apples. Another delay! By the time we reached the top, Hazel and Val were walking across one of the football pitches towards the back of the posh houses of Hinton Park. Irene had stayed with Isobel and the pram and told us that the boys had apple trees in their back garden and were giving them away. So we followed them. Being on the pitch with the big white goalposts allowed us to at least pretend we were at Wembley so we stayed on it whilst waiting for the two of them to come back with loads of apples. We couldn't take shots at goal though as the goal area was now a swamp after the rain, so we just practised our passing on the less wet edges of the pitch. In the distance, I could see the huddled crowd disappear through a gateway carved out of a huge hedge.

They seemed to take ages, so eventually Irene told us to watch Isobel as she was going over to get them. They'd be in for a telling-off I thought. No sooner had she started to venture after them, they appeared with arms full of apples. We ran over to them too. It's amazing how we can get excited at some fruit just because it came straight from a tree and not off a shop shelf. Val tossed me an apple and Hazel tossed Paul one. Irene wasn't interested. We were now all back together, but as we approached the pram that had been on the sloping path, we watched, almost in slow motion, it move from its standing position and go down the steep bank on the other side. There were screams and shrieks from me sisters and one of them shouted something about brakes. I was the first to get to the top of the bank to see the pram on its side at the bottom of it. Thankfully, the momentum it had gained going down the bank hadn't propelled it across the path and into the stream that was still full from the days of rain. In fact, the soggy grass at the bottom of the bank had created a kind of brake. I couldn't see Isobel till I reached the pram — she was still in it. I struggled to turn it back on to its wheels, but then me sisters took over and got it upright again. Isobel was awake and looking unfazed by her roller coaster ride. She probably wondered what the hysterics and fussing was about. Then came the post-mortem about the brakes. No one was willing to take responsibility and each declared that they thought 'the other' had put the brakes on. Irene being the eldest, added fuel by stating that me other two sisters shouldn't have gone with the boys in the first place. A row followed. A bigger row followed when we got back home to Ma — she was furious at first but then just relieved that Isobel was unharmed. Me sisters all moaned about being wet and muddy. Me and Paul moaned about not getting to the play park, but only to each other as we would have had our heads bitten off if we'd said it to me sisters or to our ma. I knew that the next trip to the park and the Banana slide wasn't going to happen any time soon!

Isobel didn't really feature too much in me life as I was at school all day and she was in bed pretty early in the evening. At weekends, I'd be outside playing or in the sitting room playing, whilst she was in the kitchen where Ma could keep an eye on her. There was no doubt that me and Paul teased her when the opportunity arose. It was our turn to have the upper hand over a sister for a change — to counter the controlling, teasing and ridicule we got from the older sisters. The one time that we were given full responsibility of looking after her (and the opportunity to pick on her) was on one of our trips to me granny's at Drumalief.

We went to Drumalief about once every three weeks, but during Da's two weeks' holiday at the beginning of August (the 'Derry fortnight'), we occasionally popped in for a short time on the way back from a trip to the beach at Portrush, Benone, Castlerock or Downhill. On this particular day we had gone to the beach at Castlerock. There was just me, Paul and Isobel who went with Ma and Da as the others had gotten too old to go on a family day out or, like Val and Hazel, were allowed to stay in Alfred Street under the auspices of Irene who was back home from Trinity for the summer.

Castlerock was a great place to go, though as usual we didn't get there till the early starters had started to leave for home. It had huge sand dunes that were so high that you couldn't see the actual beach till you were on the edge of them. If you approached the beach across the grassy farmland and the dunes, all you could see was the sky and the sea and you felt as if you were about to get to a cliff's edge rather than a dune's edge. Ma always liked to set up HQ as close to a dune as possible so as to reap the benefits of shelter from the wind that usually blew in from the Atlantic. There wasn't much wind today and the sun was warm on me skinny white body. Me and Paul spent the whole time either in the water, jumping the white frothy waves or playing football, cricket, tennis or golf on the harder sand that was far enough away from Isobel playing in the thicker, softer sand, but close enough for Ma and Da to keep an eye on us. If a ball wasn't hit properly and rolled anywhere near another day-tripper, Da was on our case straight away with his projected scolding voice and scowl. If nothing else, the repercussions of producing a stray ball was a good way to practise being accurate in the first place!

As there was little wind, we even had our tea on the beach. When it was windy, it was impossible to keep the sand out of your sandwiches, so we'd pack up and travel a couple of miles down the road to Downhill, where there were ample green picnic areas away from its own flat and open beach. The short grass was also ideal for playing cricket, and as Da was fairly relaxed away from his workplace, he would join in for a bit. I'd soak up his competitive banter as I loved it, and knew it was only on the few occasions like this that he showed this part of his personality. So, it was a bit special to eat our banana, ham or egg sandwiches, washed down by well-diluted orange squash, on the beach. By then, me and Paul had changed out of our wet swimming trunks and back into our shorts. Going back down to the water's edge was therefore not an option so we had to make do with making sandcastles with Isobel whilst Ma and Da packed up. In typical toddler fashion, Isobel knocked over each sandcastle before they had the luxury of standing proud. Annoying. We had no power to stop her as we were only feet away from Ma and Da.

By the time the car was packed again for the journey home, Ma and Da had the traditional discussion in the front seats of the Wolseley about whether to call in at Drumalief; we had to pass close to it on the way home. They would always discuss the time of day, who else might be there, if it was appropriate to call in on a weekday, how long before it would get dark and the fact that they hadn't brought any food supplies as they would normally do on a Sunday. Their barrister voices would bounce back and forth with rationale and evidence across the gearstick, but the verdict was always the same — we'd stop for a cup of tea. No visits to Drumalief would consist of just one cuppa, more like a pot, so I knew we'd have time for a game of footy on the grass outside. When we got to Drumalief, I'd noticed as Da was parking the car, that Uncle Billy had cut the grass so the pitch was primed for showing off footy skills. After me and Paul did our 'duty' by paying our respects to Granny, Uncle Billy and Aunt Jean by having a quick cup of tea and a biscuit with them, we were all set to get out on the pitch. Ma had other ideas. She'd been looking after Isobel all day on the beach and wanted a break, so she insisted that we take her out with us. Da laid down the law regarding looking after her — which meant that we'd be done for if anything happened to her. We weren't allowed to take the football with us either. Ma insisted that we'd played enough football for one day and that it wouldn't do us any harm to spend a bit of time with our baby sister. We knew she was right, so we didn't put up any fight. We took a hand each and walked out with Isobel.

It was surprisingly a nice feeling to hold her hand and have the anticipation of doing something different. It seemed like the first time I actually paid any meaningful attention to me little sister. Despite being with two older brothers who didn't interact with her to any great extent, Isobel was obviously happy to be with us and skipped along, bouncing her long red hair over her freckled face as she did so. She was on an adventure. The sun was well on its way down to its resting place beyond Limavady and the horizon in the distance, so the light that emanated from the now clouding-over skies added to the unusual situation and created excitement in our bodies. Once we got into the field, I felt an element of disappointment that our beloved freshly cut football pitch was going to waste tonight, but spotting the newly built haystack that came from the cut grass allowed me to move on from me low mood. Haystacks were always great fun to mess around on. It was also great to pick up huge handfuls with both hands and throw them at others, so that's what we did. Paul could fight back and gave as good as he got, but Isobel could barely pick up the hay and couldn't throw it for her supper. So, as usual, she became the target. We rained handful after handful on her head until she started to cry. Once again, we'd overstepped the mark and stopped in panic to pacify her, so as not to be found out by the adults or we'd be done for. We frantically brushed all the hay off her head and clothes. It wasn't an easy job as the hay stuck in her hair and into her woollen cardigan. Her crying was getting louder and more high-pitched and we were sure we were going to be found out. Suddenly, I heard Uncle Billy's pig make a noise from its enclosure. I managed to speak over her cries and get through to her that the pig was there just over the low wall and suggested going to see if it had piglets. It worked: Isobel's crying stopped and she nodded in the affirmative and pointed to the sty. A child's cry can apparently stop as quickly as it starts! We thought we did the best we could in managing to get the hay off her, and headed for the sty.

We reached the low wall and had a good look around to make sure the pig wasn't out and about. Paul got scared and said we should go back but the beginnings of another 'crocodile' cry from Isobel put paid to that idea. The stone house where the pig lived had a stable door on it; the top was wide open whilst the bottom was shut. However, we couldn't be sure that the bottom was securely shut and bolted from the inside. We made pig noises to see if it would respond and come to the door. We could hear grunting noises but there was no sign of it trying the door to get out into the muddy compound. Then we heard the piglets! They were like cappella singers only with squealing. As one started the others followed suit, though there didn't appear to be any differentiation between verses and the chorus. Luckily the sty was enough distance away from the house for the adults not to hear. Isobel started shouting "piglets" and enthusiastically pointing. She then attempted to open the gate. We had to be sure that the bottom door was bolted before entering the compound. Eventually, we decided to go in.

It was difficult to know whether to go slowly or run quickly to the door. Isobel made that decision for us and ran as fast as her little legs could go, so me and Paul had to follow suit. I had to pick her up to see over the lower door, and there they were, seven little piglets with big ma pig. Two were suckling whilst the others ran over to us squealing their heads off. We looked on in amazement; it wasn't every day we got to see real live piglets. Isobel clapped her hands with joy, earlier tears long dried up. As brilliant as it was to see them, the smell of pig muck was unbearable and we all pinched our noses between our finger and thumb. We were so captured in the moment that we forgot to check if the lower door was actually bolted from the inside. Uncle Billy must have put the bolt on the inside so that the likes of us couldn't interfere with it. Looking down for the bolt, I could see that it was bolted but not properly — the bolt was barely inside its slot, only its worn end was keeping the door closed. Paul was closest to it so I told him to push the bolt in some more, but he struggled to reach it properly as the door was up to his chest and the bolt was waist high on the other side. The piglets were going barmy by now and jumping against the door, rattling it in the process. Isobel got frightened and wriggled out of me grasp. As I ran after her to calm her down before she'd get back inside the house, the door swung open and Paul landed on his backside. The piglets piled out; they were free for the first time! I got to the gate before Isobel and got her through it before pulling it behind me and before the piglets got out into the field. Paul had got back onto his feet and was running now, but ma pig had also got to her feet and was after him. She was obviously going to protect her piglets and was making loud grunting sounds. Luckily, she was still heavy from producing milk for her little ones and couldn't catch up with him and he got to the gate. The problem now was opening the gate wide enough for him to get out, but without the piglets getting out and having an even greater taste of freedom. If they got into the field then they'd have access to the main gate which they could easily crawl under, and access to the main road. It's incredible how quickly your mind can conjure up a series of thoughts to create an imaginary narrative in the space of a couple of seconds, whilst being involved in a panic situation such as this.

The piglets were around Paul's feet, squealing their heads off. Paul started to squeal back in fear. I don't know how we did it, but he got out and the piglets didn't. A split second after I bolted the gate there was an almighty thud as ma pig rammed it, knocking me back in the process. How were we going to explain this to Uncle Billy, never mind Ma and Da? Too late. I looked round to see where Isobel had got to, to surprisingly see Aunt Jean pick her up — she'd come out to check that everything was okay. Her face matched her words that told us two things; one, that we had been found out doing something we shouldn't have been doing, and two, that we were not to lie when telling her what had happened. I liked Aunt Jean and her kind voice and kind face, but on this occasion, she was demanding and was clearly not to be messed with. So, I told her what happened about the hay, about the piglets and the sty door. I told her as innocently but as honestly as I could. When someone is being purely authentic, it can usually be identified as such by the listener. Aunt Jean believed me and didn't ask any further questions. She got what she wanted, the truth. She then gave me and Paul a dressing-down and made us promise that we'd not go near the pig and her piglets again. Once that was done, she then turned back into me old Aunt Jean and colluded with us that she wouldn't tell Ma or Da — or Uncle Billy. We had to agree that we'd seen the piglets though, as Isobel was going on and on about them, but we'd only seen them in the sty and they hadn't got out. If Isobel said anything about them getting out, we would just say that she was exaggerating and had got overexcited. The plan worked a treat when we'd got back inside the house. Obviously as Isobel got older and more articulate, it wasn't as easy for her to be dismissed. In fact, the pendulum swung the other way, as it seemed to me that she was always believed by Ma and Da regardless if me or Paul had done any wrongdoing or not. Resentment would kick in on occasions when I wasn't in the wrong, but this was superseded by anger if some kind of blatant unfairness was apparent. Da was always quick to punish me or Paul for our 'sins' but when Isobel would do something wrong, he didn't lay a finger on her. He might tell her off but then look to Ma to extend the reprimanding, which didn't happen. Children are often cleverer than adults think, and Isobel soon latched on to this family dynamic and understandably used it to her advantage — what child wouldn't? I guess if she'd received the same treatment as me and Paul, then she probably wouldn't have been seen by us as spoiled, as a favourite, as untouchable. I was aware that close relationships with older siblings was difficult owing to the age gaps, and I guess this would be even more potent for Isobel — she didn't even have a twin to relate to.

# Chapter 13
# The Move

The following Christmas helped to bring about a sense of unity within me family, as the house was full of positive talk about the move to the new house. Me sisters asked many questions about it, including the ones that I would have asked, so it was easy to pick up information without directly seeking it. Teatimes and Sunday dinner times were usually sprinkled with new-house seasoning, and it tasted good for everyone. The new street was called Kimberley Hill. Its name wasn't the kind of name that we were used to uttering from our lips — it sounded grand. Unsurprisingly, it elevated our social status in the Four Streets even further. Having a car and a garage was an elevation above the majority in the Four Streets anyway, but moving to the higher echelons of Woodburn or Lisnagelvin, clearly exacerbated differences in status. Da was quick to share his good news with the neighbours as he'd worked hard to get to this. He'd come a long way from the tiny dwelling in Letterkenny. He wasn't the bragging type, but clearly wanted to voice his achievements. Ma was the opposite. She wanted to remain as humble and as reserved about it as much as possible, but wasn't able to contain Da on this issue.

I was grateful for all me sisters' questions about the new house over the festive season. There was no Mina and no Robin there to ask questions as they'd both already flown the Kennedy nest. Robin had got married to Jean from Eglinton when I was ten years old and already had had a baby daughter — I was an uncle. I was even a godfather too — not that I really knew what that was or meant! Mina had got married the previous year to Barry, a Londoner, who she'd met when living and working there. So there were only six of us kids left to fit into the new house.

The new house had three bedrooms like Alfred Street, so there was nothing spectacularly new there. Me and Paul would have our bunk beds in the back bedroom, Ma and Da would have a small front bedroom, whilst the four sisters would have the big front bedroom — Val and Hazel to still share their double bed and Isobel and Irene to still have the bunk beds. So far, nothing really different. Then there was the bathroom — it was upstairs! It was much smaller than Alfred Street's, but cosy. What brought the most excitement from us was the downstairs. The kitchen was now the living room, the scullery was now the kitchen and there was a dining room (posh for us) that was off the kitchen. There was no backyard; it was now the back garden, whilst at the front of the house there was a driveway and front garden. It was impossible to visualise it all. I'd seen the Woodburn houses from the school bus but was told that Kimberley Hill was different to what I'd be able to see from the bus window. A week after the Christmas decorations had come down, Da brought the news of having the keys and that there'd be a visit to the house. Irene had already gone back to Trinity College in Dublin, so she missed out on the maiden voyage to the 'New World'.

Da had collected the keys on the Friday and the following Sunday was chosen for the expedition. Of course, it wouldn't start till the Sunday rituals had been paid their homage — Sunday school, church and Sunday dinner. Hazel had luckily got to the stage of being able to miss church. Teenage-hood can bring so many rites of passage; none more so than being able to decide not to have to do what your parents had made you do for years. For me own family, these were often linked to Sunday culture — stopping going to church or stopping visiting Drumalief. By the time me and Paul came along, many of the rites of passage battles that me elder siblings had fought for were already in place. I was grateful for their pioneering work. By the time Isobel came along, her many rites of passage were merely a formality, merely happened without voice, fuss or friction. So with Hazel at home, Ma had help preparing the dinner, which meant we ate a little earlier than usual. With Val's extra pair of hands, washing up was done in no time whilst Ma got changed for the trip. By the time we all packed into the freshly washed and polished maroon Wolseley, it was one thirty in the afternoon.

That was unheard of in our family! If Sunday was allowed to play her usual tune then we would have been dancing our way to the new house near on sunset, and we wouldn't have been able to have had a proper look at it.

I knew me bearings till Da turned into Woodburn. I could now see the bungalows up close after months of seeing them from the school bus window. Me eyes could focus on neatly cut lawns that were lined with nearly bare borders that once housed roses, pansies, peonies, marigolds and geraniums during the summer; big living room windows that had baby-sized ones to the side that opened out to breathe fresh air into the central-heated houses that were also clothed in shawls of venetian blinds; rows and rows of new red brick (not like the black-speckled red brick at Drumalief); and cars that adorned the smooth concrete driveways that led to brightly coloured garage doors.

Hazel and Val were laughing at me face with me mouth wide open and me eyes popping out of their sockets in utter amazement. I could see some shops to me right as Da turned left on to a small road without any houses for a short bit, but I could clearly see a forest of pine trees and fields that bordered the whole estate to me right. He then turned into Seven Tree Road that had more bungalows on the right but had what looked like huge houses on the left. The bungalows had porches without a door and that looked odd to me. The houses meanwhile, had a small flat roof that jutted out from the house and that gave protection from the rain just outside the front door. The most remarkable thing about them was that they had red brick halfway up the front wall then had the top half of the wall skimmed over and painted in a range of colours — blue, mustard, cream or white. The apex of the roofs brought the bright coloured walls to a halt. This felt really weird, as the apex of our house in Alfred Street was at the gable. I didn't know which house or bungalow to look at; they were all different in some way or other. Then Da came to a T-junction; we'd reached Kimberley Hill. The houses looked similar to the ones on Seven Tree Road. He turned right and said we were the third last house. The row of houses were only on one side as they faced either gardens or a road opposite them. There wasn't tarmac on the road, just gravel as the estate was very new and not yet finished. The builders were still building the bungalows on Cranford Crescent opposite on the right. It felt like Christmas morning all over again. I didn't know what delights awaited me and didn't know what presents were inside the red brick and bright-coloured wrapping paper. The third-last house was painted white, with a bright blue garage door next to it in perfect contrast. We were on a steep hill that led to a farmer's hedge only two houses further up. I could see cows in the field — wow, it felt like we were moving to the country. Da pulled up on the pavement outside the three-foot-high wall that protected the muddy earth — that would eventually become the lawn. I couldn't understand why Hazel and Val weren't as excited as me, until they confessed that they had taken a walk to it a week earlier, but hadn't said anything to anyone else. It must be great to be big I thought; you could do lots of things that you couldn't do aged eleven.

Da shouted for us to wait outside the white wrought-iron gate that crossed the front of the driveway, whilst he locked up the car. I stood there with me hand on the cold latch until Da was near enough the gate so that I wouldn't be given a slap for disobeying his order. I sprung it open and ran up the driveway, touching the white fence that separated it from next door's garden, then the garage door and then the metal pole that supported the flat overhang roof outside the front door. Everything was different and new to me. Of course, the big moment was Da opening the front door. He took his time, enjoying the drama of the occasion, just as he'd done when driving down Alfred Street to announce me and Paul being born. I could see that he was pleased with himself, his face was relaxed and his eyes showed their friendliness that friends and acquaintances always got to see.

In I ran. Where shall I go first? There was no lino or carpet on the hallway floor to the right or on the staircase that was straight ahead of me. The stairs spoke the loudest as they always did with their whispers of mystery in the background, so up I ran. Paul followed. The indoor bathroom hit me first at the top of the stairs, with its toilet, sink and bath. It was tiny compared to the one in Alfred Street, but it was new. Next was the back bedroom, our room. The big window looked out on to the top soil of a back garden with a high banking at its back that was then topped by a bull wire fence to separate it from ours. Beyond that was a cow's field that hadn't been dug up yet for more houses, but to its left were half-built houses that would eventually spread their way across the unspoilt field. There was a wardrobe that was hidden in the wall like a secret passage from an Agatha Christie novel. The shorter door in the middle of the landing just showed the water tank and hot press — boring. Then the big front bedroom that would house me sisters. It was twice the size of ours and had a sliding door that led to another secret wardrobe — amazing. The huge window gave a fantastic view across fields and more half-built houses, but beyond these were hills straight ahead. Then a look to the right showed the rooftops of Woodburn houses and beyond them in the distance was the Derry side. I could see the houses of Creggan, and beyond them, the mountains of Donegal. I wanted this view and not the restricted one from me own bedroom, but I consoled meself with the thought that I'd come in here as often as possible to take a look out of this window. Being at the top of Kimberley Hill was a far cry from the bottom of Alfred Street. Perhaps the oppressive darkness would be no more, I thought.

Next door was the small bedroom that was to be Ma and Da's. It was really small and I wondered why they chose this room as theirs and not ours. Again, there was a sliding door that hid a secret wardrobe in the wall. It was impossible to imagine living here as the floorboards were still uncovered and the walls were still showing the smooth skimming plasterwork of the plasterers. The smell was a mixture of wood and plaster.

I ran downstairs and found a space under the stairs off the hallway — in Alfred Street, that space was part of the kitchen! Then into the kitchen with an adjoining dining room, separated by a huge rectangular opening. Ma was fiddling with the new electric cooker with metal rings at the top; it had been fitted since she'd last visited. Of course, there was no flame like our gas cooker so it was difficult to know if it was working or not. Ma touched a ring and duly burned her finger. This was a lesson for all of us. We then stood around in amazement to watch all four rings eventually turn to red. I couldn't figure out how it all worked but soon lost interest and opened a large cupboard door that showed a number of shelves. I was told it was the larder, for keeping food in. The adjoining dining room had nothing really to investigate in it, so I went through another door that led to the living room. It was a big room with a fireplace and hearth, with tiles and a mantelpiece that were a more modern version of the ones in our sitting room. The ginormous window looked out into the front and the rest of the street; I'd never seen a window so big! At an angle, I could see a glimpse of the Donegal Mountains. The Tins were nowhere in sight. I couldn't see anywhere obvious that would become me new playground, me new Wembley, me new Western Front, me new Wild West, me new place to escape to. The cow field to the left was the only option right now, but they had cows in them!

Over the coming weeks, the physical, mental and emotional transition from Alfred Street, the Four Streets and the Tins, to Kimberley Hill took place. Da borrowed a small trailer from someone from his work and me and Paul made what seemed like hundreds of trips in the evenings and Saturdays with him to Kimberley Hill. We started with the garage and shed where Da had stored many tools, many pieces of wood and bits of metal over the years. We filled the trailer and the boot of the car and then filled up the new garage with the old stuff. Each trip allowed me to see the new house looking more liveable, as the painters brought the door frames, the skirting boards, the ceilings and the walls to life; albeit with soulless white paint. I spent less time with me mates during this transition period. It was dark by the time I'd get home from school, whilst the Tins were always more out of bounds during the winter months anyway. Whereas Saturdays were spent with Da, Paul and the trailer. I was moving away from all that I'd known, without really being aware of it. Friends, people, places, things are all temporary in our lives, no matter how close we become to them or how meaningful they are to us at any given time. We adapt, like all species, to new ground, new territory, new experiences. Maybe adapting to this change was me own subconscious way of dealing with loss?

The day of the move soon came. It was a Wednesday, a school day, so me mates were not around. In fact, I don't remember really saying goodbye to them. There was no rain. Me and Paul were told to play outside with our football, and we did for a bit, but then sat on the sleepers that fenced the Tins for one last time and watched the removal men carry all our furniture and belongings out of the house and into the huge van. It was like seeing our whole house, our lives, be exposed to all who stood around watching — there were plenty of spectators. That intrusion didn't feel right so I wanted the men to finish emptying the house as fast as possible. It seemed no time before they had loaded everything up and Da called us to get in the car. I had one last look over me shoulder at the Tins, before seeing two helicopters rise into the air from the barracks to see us off.